The Pursuit of Man

Genesis

Matthew Rings

CROSSBOOKS

CrossBooks™
A Division of LifeWay
1663 Liberty Drive
Bloomington, IN 47403
www.crossbooks.com
Phone: 1-866-879-0502

© 2012 Matthew Rings. All rights reserved.

No part of this book may be reproduced, stored in a retrieval system, or transmitted by any means without the written permission of the author.

First published by CrossBooks 09/18/2012

ISBN: 978-1-4627-1914-3 (sc)
ISBN: 978-1-4627-1915-0 (e)

Library of Congress Control Number: 2012917481

Printed in the United States of America

Any people depicted in stock imagery provided by Thinkstock are models, and such images are being used for illustrative purposes only.

Certain stock imagery © Thinkstock.

Because of the dynamic nature of the Internet, any web addresses or links contained in this book may have changed since publication and may no longer be valid. The views expressed in this work are solely those of the author and do not necessarily reflect the views of the publisher, and the publisher hereby disclaims any responsibility for them.

Acknowledgements

I would like to thank my wife for supporting me and putting up with my craziness and me all these years.

I would like to thank my daughters for helping me with this devotional.

I would also like to give props to Greg Marshall.

I would like to thank Austin Koon for sending me that prodding text to finish this book.

Thanks to Lorraine Rings for helping me with this book.

Thanks Paul for putting up with me when I was an obnoxious teenager!

I would like to thank my mom for giving me a Godly example

Finally, this book is dedicated to all the students that God has allowed me to be your shepherd/sheepdog.

Introduction

I could write a prequel to this Journey through scripture titled "Man's run from God" thus the need for this book. Throughout scripture, we are continually being dim witted and defiant and running from the only one who truly loves us unconditionally. By the way, when I say man, it's not a gender reference but link to huMAN. Which is you, unless you're a really gifted monkey or dolphin, in which case you should put this book down and back away slowly and go play with your ball.

When people tell me "I run 3 miles a day," I usually respond, "I run only when chased." It always gets a cheap laugh, but maybe that joke is more profound than it ought to be. Maybe God pursues us, chases us because we continue to run. Why else does he keep telling us in scripture to "be still?" If only we would be still in God's presence, the intimacy with God that awaits us is beyond fathoming. I hope that is what we will do together over these chapters on our journey through God's Word. Speaking of which, this book is a companion to be read along with a chapter of the Genesis each day. Read the Bible passage first and then this book or vice versa, try both approaches and see what you like. I prefer the New Living Translation as it is accurate and easy to read and understand, which I think are good qualities to have.

It's hard for us sometimes to savor the Bible and explore deeper because of our familiarity of the events. I tried to block out any memory of what happens next and read each chapter with freshness to see what God was doing in the lives of His people step by step.

We all know Abraham and Joseph's story. We know how it ends and our minds often rush over passages without chewing our food slowly and enjoying the flavor. For me, this journey through scripture in the pursuit of man is like an Outback Steak. When I get the filet, I take small bites and chew slowly enjoying the flavor and texture of the finest steak in the land. My hope is you will walk away from this book with that approach to reading God's word. As you read the lives of real people, savor the aroma of their lives, their culture, the customs, and the geography. All these angles come together to take you deeper in the lives of the people you read about here in Genesis. Savoring a passage, putting yourself in the culture with a teleporting time machine will turn scripture from a dry and dusty ancient scroll into a 3-D action movie with God and his people as the stars. Watch and see how God's plan of redemption explodes off the pages as God pursues his people.

My hope for you and for me throughout this journey through scripture is that you could see the relentless pursuit of God. I hope you will see how God is connected to the folks here in Genesis, but also I hope you find great solace that God is pursuing you. The Bible is no man made story about God, it's too messy and we look like fools too often. This is God's story, a story of redemption, love and God's passionate pursuit of man.

2 Quick things: **1.** Sometimes I get a **RANDOM THOUGHT**, so I just say whatever pops into my head and when my random thought is over you will see this **THGUOHT MODNAR. 2.** There is a phrase "Where the rubber meets the road," it means here is the most important point for something or the moment of truth or time to get into action. An athlete can train all day, but the race is where the "rubber meets the road" and they'll know how good they really are. So in keeping with our theme of running I thought it would only be appropriate to take a few moments after you read a passage to ask the question "What does this mean and How can I apply this to my life" So at the end of each chapter there are questions to put our bodies and hearts in motion. When reading God's Word there needs to be a response. How can I go forward and live this out?

Diorama Dirt Ball earth

(Remember to Read Genesis chapter 1)

In the beginning **BAM!** Out of darkness came an explosion of light bigger than any special effects we have ever seen! How cool is it that the very thing God begins *HIS*tory with is the same thing that He ends it with! The Light. Did you catch that play on words? History, time, space, it's all God's story, it's all about the glory of God, a.k.a. **HIS** story revealed to us through His Word to us. The Bible is God revealing Himself to us, not the other way around. When God speaks, amazing things happen, as we see here in Genesis! So look with expectancy to His Word to you here in Bible.

The Light. Jesus tells folks, "I am the light of the world. If you follow me, you won't have to walk in darkness, because you will have the light that leads to life" (John 8:12). Saving sinners out of darkness and out of shame is what God's story is all about. This book we call the Bible is the story of God's wild, passionate love for his people. It is a story from cover to cover of our redemption and so there is no better way to begin than by light bursting on to the scene to begin God's story of his pursuit of man.

God is busy at work or probably more like play for Him creating all the various rivers, mountains animals and human life in His shoebox diorama we call Earth.

Later we see that God has "measured off the heavens with His fingers." (Isaiah 40:12) And David looks up at the stars at night as he sheps and says in Psalm 19" The heavens declare the Glory of God, the skies proclaim the work of His hands. This gives you a glimpse of the vastness of God and our itty bittyness.

RANDOM THOUGHT 1:29 some people, mostly vegans like to point to this verse and say "Ah ha!" see Adam and Eve only had plants and vegetables to eat so God wanted us all to be vegan! But we know that is not true because of the great theologian Homer. No not the one with mythology, Homer Simpson "If God didn't want us to eat animals he wouldn't have made them out of meat."

THGUOHT MODNAR

Look around you today and notice the glory of God's creativity in creation. What does the creation story here in Genesis 1 reveal about God's character? Take a minute to talk to God in prayer and thank Him for the little things you notice in creation and the big Amazing things too.

West and Wewaxzation

(Don't forget to read Genesis Ch 2)

God had been busy @ work for 6 days and He was slap wore out so He had to take a break. Seriously?? Have you ever been so exhausted after making a diorama you had to take a whole day to recoup? Come on man, they aren't that hard! God wasn't exhausted and didn't **need** a break. He simply rested to model for us a pattern of work and rest. A healthy combo we have a real hard time balancing in our lives. Being a workaholic is a way of life for adults and especially teenagers today. Teenagers are juggling sports, grades, kung fu music lessons (they are so short on time they have to mix the two!) not mention church, family and friends. We **need** a rest! We need to stop all our craziness for one day and simply be still.

Our day of rest today is usually Sunday for most folks, but we need to be careful to not lose the "Why" behind the command to rest. Yeah our bodies need a break, but it's not just about that, our day of rest should also have the element of reconnecting with God and worshiping Him. God models this concept of rest here for us in Gen 2:1-3 and later makes it part of his top 10 list to make sure we see the importance of resting.

The rest of this chapter is telling us some of the details of what God did in creation back in Gen 1. Chapter 2:18-20 always cracks me up! God made all the animals and they each had a mate, but Adam was alone and this is the first time we see God say something was not good. This is one of those passages you can easily skim over and miss is you aren't paying attention to the details. But if you read this paragraph in its context there is something funny going on. I'm pretty sure God was messing with Adam here and having some fun. So imagine with me the context. Man is alone, needs a mate and then God begins to bring the animals He created to Adam to name/ look for a mate.

So God gets out his play-doh and begins making things. He makes something about 17 feet tall with 6-foot long legs and about a 6-foot long neck. God brings this creature to Adam and he says "Aaaa, what-da-ya think?" And Adam looks with his one eyebrow raised and says, "Yeah, I don't think that's going to work out, let's just call that one a giraffe." And God says, "Ok, fair enough, let's try this one. Next up let's try something a little smaller, here's a few spiky things to make it fun." And Adam crinkles up his nose and says "Yeah, that's defiantly not going to work, let me just call that one a porcupine . . . Next" And on and on each new animal went by and nada. The context of Adam being alone in the beginning of this paragraph down to verse 20 that says there was still no helper just right for him.

A lot of people look at verse 19-20 as separate and it was just Adam naming all the animals, but it was God bringing animals by to see if Adam could find a date! (For those of you still dating/ waiting to find a perfect mate I know you can relate to the platypus and porcupines that you come across in the whole dating scene :)

So after the zoo parade God knocks Adam out and makes him something beautiful. As Adam wakes up and his eyes come into focus from the anesthesia he sees before him a beautiful naked creature and his response was "Whoa Man! I'll take one please! She will be called woman."

RANDOM THOUGHT Verse 25 is one of my favorite verses to write on the back of my friend's car windshield with shoe polish at their wedding day. Feel free to use that at your next friend's wedding.

THGUOHT MODNAR

Since you are made in God's image, how does your life reflect Him?

How does the fact that people are made in God's image affect the way you feel about yourself?

Hide-n-Go-Seek

From the beginning of God's story in Genesis we see God create man & woman and He says in chapter 1:31 that now, everything is "Very good." God delighted in us, He loved us and longed to be with us. After the account of God creating us in Gen 2, we come to the fall of man into sin. This is the part of the story where we blew it. We get a glimpse of what the relationship was like in Gen 3:8a. Can you feel the cool breeze across you face and hear the lush jungle leave gently dancing like wind before a cleansing rain?

Here we see God going for a walk in the garden and I have to believe that this was a regular and probably a daily event. God would come and hang out with his children that he is wildly in love with. I'm sure they spent time together laughing and God spent a lot of time answering questions. I'm sure Adam and Eve were always asking questions like "What is that? Oooh what is this shinny thing?" Whatever they talked about, the picture of intimacy untainted is sweet in the evening breeze.

But we get to 8b and the "Game is afoot" as Mr. Holmes used to say; the cosmic game of Hide-and-go-seek. We've all been there, hiding from God thinking He can't see us. When my daughter Kaleigh was 3 she loved to play hide-n-go seek like every kid. But at 3 she wasn't very good at coming up with new places to hide, so sometimes she would run from me while I was counting and when I came to find her I would call out "Where's Kaleigh, where did she go?" And she would giggle uncontrollably but maintained her hiding spot, which was in the middle of the floor in plain view! :) She was tucked up in a ball with her face to the floor and hands over her eyes giggling. As far as she was concerned, she couldn't see me, so I couldn't see her. Kids are so much fun, goofy, but fun!

When I read this account of God walking in the garden calling out "Where are you?" I'm reminded of the game my daughter and I played. God is Omni-everything so of course He knew where they were **and** what they had done, but he still pursued them. I just have to say, I crack up every time I read verse 11. I'm not sure if it's meant to be funny, but what a great question. "Who told you you were naked?" Busted! They were nakie before, but it didn't matter; now they've told on themselves!

Adam begins the blame game and I can feel God's heart rip as His beloved children begin to turn their backs on God in defiance and turn on Him and blame God. There are consequences for our actions and God is clear with Adam and Eve on the cost of their defiance. The crazy thing is immediately after God disciplines His children by casting them out of the garden, He does something amazing look at verse 21. God looked at the ridiculous outfit of twigs and leaves that had to be uncomfortable and God lovingly made them something more Comfortable from soft animal fur. We see the shedding of blood for us as a foreshadowing of Jesus blood shed for us to take away our sin. It's all right here in the beginning! We blow it and God's immediate response is to provide a loving way to redeem His beloved people. The same thing is true for you and me when we mess up. When we confess our mistakes, a.k.a. sin, God is faithful to lovingly restore us and we are forgiven because of who Jesus is and what He has done for us.

When have you been tempted to hide from God today? Take a minute to tell God about the messed up stuff in your heart, a.k.a. sin, you may have been involved in and ask God to forgive you, cleanse you, and set you apart ready to start fresh.

Sibling Rivalries 4

If you are like me and like to read first thing in the morning, this chapter's first sentence will wake you up! Adam had sex with Eve. Hello, I wasn't ready for that. This being the first time a couple did that, there was no one to warn them of the results of having "relations." Anyway, the next 9 months must have been pretty weird as Eve's belly grew Adam was probably freaking out! What is going on?? What is happening to her belly?! I don't think Eve was freaked out as much because women have this intuition about these kinds of things and probably figured out it wasn't a watermelon seed that she swallowed like Adam insisted.

RANDOM THOUGHT—Did Adam and Eve have belly buttons? This is debated all across the world and for 1000's of years in churches and seminaries, it has divided churches and started the Spanish inquisition! Ok, I made that whole last sentence up, but there is no way Adam & Eve had belly buttons! They had smooth bellies like a Ken doll with no lint catchers. Deal with it, it's a scientific fact that no time in a belly = no extension cord to cut = no button.

THGUOHT MODNAR

Back to our Text. Verse 2—I wish I could be a shepherd someday maybe just for a weekend. (If you have sheep and you could make me an honorary shepherd, you should email me!) I think I could shep and enjoy it. Talk about foreshadowing God's master plan of loving us sheep and rescuing us, here it is with shepherds. Do you remember what David did as a teenager while he wrote all those hit worship songs? (Psalms are songs by the way :)) He was a shepherd hanging out with sheep looking at the vastness of the stars at night.

What about the first guys to hear about Jesus birth? The Messiah, our rescuer is here . . . Shepherds. Check out Luke 2 and see God revealing Himself to the shepherds.

The life of Able & Cain is short and sad. This is the first family ever, so what went wrong? Did Adam spend too much time at the office neglecting the proper training of the boys? Was Eve too busy shopping and working out at the YMCA neglecting Cain's emotional needs? They didn't have the crazy hurried life style we have today; they weren't distracted by TV, computers, texting etc . . . Yet they were still messed up! Why?? Why couldn't this simple family of 4 love each other, get along and not be jealous and envious? God tells Cain why in verse 7 "sin is crouching @ the door eager to control you." Just like Peter warns us to "Stay alert! Watch out for your great enemy, the devil. He prowls around like a roaring lion, looking for someone to devour." (1 Peter 5:8) The reason is sin. When we let sin become our master, it consumes us and destroys our lives. So we need to guard our hearts to keep us out of trouble.

For whatever reason, our families are one of the hardest places to keep peace. It could be the daily exposure to each other or the careful study of what gets on your brother/sisters nerves (Which was the case for me). I would watch and see what set my sister off, and if she messed with me, I would push that button to set her off. Maybe it was a hurtful comment or teasing and tearing her down emotionally. I would push her to the point that she became angry and then she would pounce upon me like a lion and beat the crap out of me! (Don't laugh! She was 3 years older than me and that girl was tough!) You would think I would have learned my lesson and kept my mouth shut, but alas, I am slow and dim witted.

As we grew up together there was this vicious cycle of insults usually followed by physical violence like the 3 Stooges, where I was on the receiving end of a coke bottle over my head or being kicked through my window shutters. Why? Why was my sister so mean to me? Why couldn't I keep my mouth shut? It wasn't my sister's fault entirely; it was our sin nature rearing its ugly head. I wish I would have studied God's word and looked at this first sibling rivalry and learned from God's warning when I was a wee lad. I wish I had seen the wrong done to me and instead of amplifying it to a point where my sin became my master; I would have done the right thing. I wish

I could have done the Godly thing and loved her and not stirred up trouble.

Sin. It manifests itself in many ways in our lives and it is what pushed Cain to the point of killing his brother. Sin is the reason I pushed my sister with my hurtful words and it is by God's grace alone that I lived to make it through my childhood! It is sin that is wreaking havoc in your life as well if you are not careful with your family. Be careful with your words and guard your hearts so that sin doesn't consume you and ruin your family. Whether its siblings or your relationship with parents, beware, sin is crouching waiting to ruin and devour. Maybe you're reading this now and realize that it's time to stop living in strife and warfare with your brother or sister or parents for that matter. I hope you will learn from my mistakes and Cain's and do the right thing.

At the end of Gen 4, there is a sentence that a first you blaze right over 4:26b. But it struck me that when Adam & Eve had their grandson Enoch from Seth they "began to worship the Lord by Name." Yehova is the proper name of God here and to me it shows the intimacy between God and his people. This is no sterile deity or cosmic fairy tale; it is a mutual love story between God and His children respond to His love with worship.

How is your family like Adam, Eve, Cain & Able? What is good in your family? Take a minute to tell your mom/dad/brother/sister what you've read and ask them to forgive you for any hurtful stuff in the past. Pray and ask God to help your family avoid some of these hurtful conflicts.

5 Martians??

I do **it** all the time and I know you do **it** to, but try to not do **it** anymore. What is "**it**?" It= is seeing a genealogy in scripture and FFWD past it. We see it and we say "here we go again" some dude had relations and had a kid named Vuvuzela or some weird name you can't pronounce and so you skip over it to get to the "good stuff." Try not to do **it**; there is good stuff in the history of God's story unfolding in the lives of people.

For example, if you saw this genealogy and skipped over to chapter 6, you would have missed a really cool story of Enoch in verse 22 Enoch lived in close fellowship with God for another 300 years and then God took him! Why? Where did he go?

Looking at this long list of begetters, I find it intriguing that God didn't just cast humans aside and move on to one of the other billions of planets out there and make a new creature race that wasn't so disobedient and always wanted to worship him. Or maybe He did! Do de do do, do de do do!?? I'm just kidding, or am I? But seriously, instead of God giving up on us, we see His love for us and in return, we have the desire to worship God by name. By the time we get to Gen 6 we can see God's patience had been tested by his bratty and now increasingly wicked creation—humans.

Check your footnotes in you bible if you have them and look for any place in scripture Enoch is mentioned. I'll help you with this one; check out Hebrews 11:5. He went to be with God because he was known as a person that pleased God. Wow! How awesome is that! When people talk about you, is that what they say? When they look at your life, do they say _____ lives their life to please God? I hope you would live your faith out loud in a way that people notice and it touches the lives of those God has placed around you. Take a minute and ask God to use you today so that people will see God evident in your life.

Noah, He built him an Arky Arky

We see God zoom in on the one guy who verse 9 tells us "walked in close fellowship with God." There is that image again from the garden with the cool wind blowing and God walking and talking with Noah. Looking at the story of the flood may seem like God is not concerned about man or He wouldn't kill them all. But, the truth is **because** God loved man and had let him run wild for far too long there needed to be a cleansing. So God, in his justice and mercy choose Noah to make a fresh start.

When I go to fix something in my house, toilet, closet door, wood flooring, whatever. I will visit Lowes or Home Depot usually 4 times as a minimum just for that one project. Usually it's 1 time to buy "everything I need" for the project and then 3 more times in one day just to get what I forgot. I once went to Lowes, bought what I needed for the project, and went to my car to sit and think so I wouldn't have to come back. Of course I remembered something and went back in to get it . . . 4 times I did this and the cashier just laughed at me everything I came back inside. I can't imagine how long it would have taken me to build an ark like Noah did. This massive Zooboat was built without a single trip to Lowes! Well done sir!

RANDOM THOUGHT

Some people don't believe Noah and the Ark actually existed. They think it's just a fable but that is not the case if you believe the Bible is the authentic word of God. There is no room for legends or fairy tales or mythological stories found in the Bible. Your view of God's word, the Bible matters. It is either %100 factual historical account of our beginning and God's involvement in their lives or it is %100 lie. You can't have fairy tales mixed with theology. There is a ton of geological and scientific evidence that points to a flood, but that is just the icing on the cake. As a Christian, you read God's story and you see God to be truthful and trust worthy. So when someone comes along and says science has confirmed the Biblical account of blah blah blah that's nice, but we already knew God's word to us in the Bible istrue.

THGUOHT MODNAR

If you were alive when the flood happened, why would God choose you?

A. Because you like puppies?
B. He has to choose somebody
C. you try your best to be a good person
D. you don't think he would
E. God is gracious

God decided He would love you and draw you to Himself out of pure Grace. Thank Him for that today.

Old Dudes Rule!

So Noah finally finished the boat and had all the animals together and it is my guestamate that it took him 100 years. Now you may say 100 years! Seriously, could these people not count or did they have a bad calendar? No, if you read Ch5 you see the life span of people was a lot longer the closer to creation you get. Maybe it's like the whole dog year thing we somehow calculated for every year we live today it is like 7 years for a dog. I think today you and I are the dogs who age quicker.

Do the math, if we live to be 100 today that would be like Noah and them living to 700. I don't believe they were all old and wrinkled like Yoda at age 80 like we get today. I think it was a lot longer life and they really lived hundreds of years and aged slower. The reason I think it took Noah at least 100 years is 5:32 says Noah was 500 when he had his 3 sons, who had to help him build the yacht. And by the time Noah was 600 7:6 God told him to get on the Boat.

Another cool thing is chapter 6 verse 20. Noah and his family didn't have to travel all over and live capture 2 of every animal. God made the animals come to Noah, which is quite helpful!

Verse 10 is funny. After 100 years of building a boat in the desert and funny looks from the neighbors, God says all aboard. Then they wait and wait and wait. I wonder if the neighborhood kids came by and made fun of Noah and his family inside the massive cruise ship for 7 days.

Have you ever had to wait on God? What was the result of that wait? Hebrews 11:7 tells us that Noah is known as a man of faith because he waited patiently on the Lord. In the introduction, I told you about the phrase "When the rubber meets the road" Here we see Noah's faith be more than a religious ideal, he put it in action and obeyed God. What about you?

The rain rain rain came down down down

Have you ever been cooking something like Mac-n-cheese, you're watching something good on TV or playing a video game, and you are going "back and forth" from the kitchen to your show. But then the show gets interesting and you go "forth" from the kitchen, but you forget to go "back." You're engaged in your show and then 20 min later you remember you were cooking something and run back to the kitchen to find your delicious Mac-n-cheese is now crusty and burnt. You forgot to remember! I do it all the time. I was gonna try to take those vitamins, I can't remember the name of them that help you remember stuff, but I couldn't remember to take them . . . wait, where am I? Who are you?? And why are you reading my memoirs??? Oh wait, now I remember, sorry I forgot what I was doing for a second. Anyway, fortunately chapter 8 begins with great words of encouragement! "God remembered." God isn't off making a new galaxy or watching his 72 billion mile wide screen TV, He is every present in the lives of those He loves. He remembers. Always! Genesis tells us God remembered Noah and all the animals, how awesome is that! I don't know what tough stuff you have been through lately but for me to know my God remembers me is huge.

I haven't been through a worldwide apocalyptic flood to understand the depths of Noah and his families fear together, but I have been through some "deep waters" of life and they were hard. As the great theologian Bono once said "I was drowning my sorrow, but my sorrows, they learned to swim."

I don't know if you have ever felt that way, but life can be tough. I have been in that dark place where it felt like the world was coming to an end and the thing that sustained me and will sustain you is the same thing that kept Noah afloat. God remembered Noah, He remembers me in my time of despair, and the millions of others before and after me and He remembers you. Rest assured in the knowledge that our God is not forgetful.

A lot of people mistakenly think this ordeal was 40 days of rain and then it was all over. 40 days of rain is nothing! It rains 154 days a year in Seattle every year. Look at chapter 8 verses 13-14 it tells us they were on this boat for **a year!** The springs and heavy rains all attributed to the massive flood. So this whole ordeal of building the boat and gathering animals, waiting for the rain, and waiting for God to draw back the waters was about 1 year according to my calculations. Which even according to my dog year theory, 7 years of tough times is a long time. *((BTW Don't freak out about the whole dog years thing, it's just for fun and not meant to be a factual biblically accurate philosophy.)) I say all that to help you step back from the hard stuff you might be struggling with to see it from a "doves eye view" (8:6-12). God knows the flood that has consumed you; he is able to draw the waters down. He alone will provide for your physical, emotional and spiritual needs through the deep floods of your life. He will bring you back to dry land don't give up hope. (BTW if you ever need someone to pray for you, email me and I will pray with you through your flood matthewrings@gmail.com)

I love verse 20! You know all throughout this ordeal Noah was praying, talking to God, and as soon as he steps off the boat he builds an alter to worship the God who sustained him. God makes a covenant with Himself in 21 that even though we are sinful from birth God will love us, protect us, and not destroy us.

What is something hard that God is asking you to do? How can God's faithfulness to remember Noah be an encouragement to you?

Somewhere over the rainbow

We find God making the first "Covenant" with Noah and his family and all the animals. God has promised to never flood the entire earth again so Noah and his family don't run in fear when it rains.

So Noah is commanded to have relations with his wife and make lots of baby's. I like that verse 3 commands him to eat steak and potatoes, sorry vegans. God is giving Noah the basic guidelines to survive and start this whole thing over, new and fresh. God gives them another of his top 10 list items here. Remember back in Gen 2 he gives them the command to rest and here is another one "do not murder." Why not? Because "to kill a person is to kill a living being made in God's image." What in the world does that mean? We saw it back in Gen 1:27 but I wanted to save it till now to look at it.

Does it mean we physically look like God? My daughters bear my image; they each have a physical feature that I have passed down to them that my pappy had and his pappy before him. Is that what it means? Does God have hair (or a small bald spot like me), eyes, two big toes, opposable thumbs or what about a belly button?! The answer is . . . I have no idea. I know He doesn't have a belly button, but it's possible that God gave us features that are similar to His since we were made in His image. Of course, God is infinite and spirit etc and any bodily form he may have would be infinitely perfect. No pimples and no pot belly, but it isn't exactly like our bodies that have a born on date and an expiration date. These "tents" as Paul calls them are just that, temporary homes here on planet earth.

Or maybe being made in God's image is about our emotional and spiritual souls. The way we have feelings of love and sorrow, compassion, anger, forgiveness. These are all character traits that set us apart as creatures made in the image of God. The bottom line is we don't know what features we have that make us look like our Father, but it makes us unique. It makes you unique that God has designed you and created you to be in His image. That is why He loves humans deeper than anything else He created. You have your Fathers eyes and heart and He is wildly in love with you! It's also and why life is sacred and not to be taken.

Verse 9 God makes a covenant with Noah to never send another flood. A covenant is described by dictionary.com as "an agreement, usually formal, between two or more persons to do or not do something specified." Marriage is supposed to be a great example of that when we stay true to the commitment. When a man looks into the eyes of his schmoopsie-poo and she looks into the eyes of her googlie bear (Monsters Inc) at the church and they declare their undying love for each other. They commit to being together for as long as they both shall live. That is an agreement between 2 parties to keep their promise. What sets a covenant apart from a sterile legal contract is often a more intimate emotional investment in the marriage covenant and a loving compassionate connection when God makes a covenant with His people.

The funny thing about this covenant with Noah and some other covenants that God makes is the parties involved. Take a second and re-read 8-17 again and tell me who the 2 parties are in this agreement? Go ahead, I'll wait right here . . . Welcome back, did you figure it out? If you said between God and Noah, congratulations, you're wrong! :) This promise/agreement/covenant is between the only parties that are capable of keeping their end of the deal.

Why was there a flood? Oh yeah, mankind had become wicked and corrupt and deceitful. So we couldn't be trusted to keep our end of the contract so God made a covenant with Himself on our behalf. The reason I say it's between God and Himself is in a normal contract between 2 parties if one person does something to break that contact, then the promise/agreement/covenant is null and void. So if that is the case when you read 8-17 what is it that Noah has to do to keep his end of the deal? Nada! God doesn't say if you're good boys and girls, I will give you a rainbow and if you break your end of the deal, you had better get your swimmies on!

God promises us that He will never flood the earth again and God is not forgetful. The covenant was made on our behalf so every time we see a rainbow or a "Whooooa Double Rainbow" we are to remember that we have a gracious God who loves us and cares for us.

What are 2 things you have learned about God's character in this chapter?

Why does God make such a big deal about not taking another human's life?

In light of verse 6, how does this affect your view on abortion?

Really Old Spice

Here **it** is again, another genealogy I hope you resisted the temptation to FFWD. These are not unimportant nobodies who we don't know. I know they aren't taught in Vacation Bible School and they don't have their own felt board action figures, but they are important. As you read through chapter 10 and on through to 11:14 we find some guy named Shelah. And here in the beginning of scripture we see the pattern again of God knowing us personally. God knew that when Shelah was 30 he was going to become a daddy for the 1st time. God rejoiced in the birth of little Eder and God cared for that family and he took care of their needs. I know when my first child was born I was worried and excited and I take great comfort in this little detail of a verse that God will do the same for me and my family. He was there at my birth, pulled all-nighters to watch over and protect me from myself·in middle and high school all the way to my wedding day and on to my funeral party. He will be there for my family as they grieve and rejoice through life and the same promise is true for you and your life.

I bought a bottle of Old Spice body wash recently and for some reason I was in the shower and looked at the back of the bottle. What I read made me laugh really loud which made my wife question my sanity . . . even further, but I think it applies here as we ebb towards father Abraham. The bottle read, and I quote "Old Spice, if your grandfather hadn't worn it, you wouldn't exist." The same thing is true for 'ol Abraham. If his great-great-great-great-great-grand pappy hadn't used Old Spice Ur Breeze edition we wouldn't have known father Abraham or his many sons or that I am one of them and we never would have learned the Abraham hooky Poky in VBS! Thank you Lord for Old Spice Ur Breeze!

What is something you can do to celebrate/ acknowledge your family heritage?

What is one way you can demonstrate respect for your parents this week?

Famine & Flocks of Goats

Next up we have the zoom lens out again for the life of Abram aka Abraham. 12:2 God tells Abram I will make you into a great nation, I will bless you and make you famous and you will be a blessing to others. God comes to Abram again and again with a simple pattern. God says Abram I want you to _____ and Abram responds in faithfulness and God blesses his sandals off. Here we see God say I want you to leave your country and family and go. Abram doesn't even know where it is he is going, he just knew God said go and when you get there I'll tell you. You and I want a Google map and GPS coordinates before we travel across town and we often take the same approach toward God. God may be pressing on your heart "I want you to go." Maybe it's on a short-term mission trip or into full time ministry or even just go to your next-door neighbor or that person at work or school and invest in their lives. God may be saying, "I want you to go and share my amazing story with them." "Just Go" he says, but we freak out if we don't have a detailed plan and often we live in disobedience to God's simple call to **Go**.

God said to Abram I want you to go and Abram starts packing and because of his faithful response to God's call, God blesses Abram. Abram responds in worship, and God delights in his heart, and God blesses him more. BTW, this isn't some secret formula for wealth and prosperity. It is the beautiful pattern of a love relationship and a life that is showing a heart for God, and God's heart for man.

What is God calling you to step out in Faith and trust Him to lead you in?

Take a minute to ask God to take control of your future and give it to Him to lead you wherever He calls. Commit to God that you will follow Him wherever He leads you like Abram.

13 Worship

We see Lot and Abram part ways here and we begin to see this love relationship between Abram and God grow deeper. Abram reciprocates God's love by stopping and worship God again for His faithfulness in protecting Abram and Sari in Egypt. (Verse 4) The rest of the chapter tells us of how God blesses little lot(all grown up now) and I love the way chapter 13 ends the way it began . . . in Worship.

We were born to worship! We love to worship, just look at the fans of the latest Pop Star. From Elvis to Michael Jackson to whatever teen band is at the top 40 this week there are millions of people around the world bowing down in worship and adoration.

However, this is no man made god or an attempt to appease a sun god or fertility god, this is a relationship of warmth and adoration that flows both ways. This is no product of man's imagination, but a revelation of God's love and compassion for His people. Wow! That should propel us into worshiping, making an alter, sacrificing and singing and adoring God.

So what is on the throne of your worship? What are you sacrificing time and your attention toward? Is it some person or rock star; is it work, or a sport or your school or relationship? Or is it you? Do you worship and adore yourself so much there is no room for God?

The Dark Night 14

It's nice to have a mini army of 318 men around when trouble brews. So when Abram and his army snuck in the dark of night they delivered swift justice for kidnapping Lot. It's also nice to have the God of the universe as your ally when you're fighting any of the "ites." Hittites, Amorites, and Mosquitobites . . . (Bud dump dump ting. Sorry I couldn't resist that one)

And so we come to the mysterious Melchizedek. Where did a high priest come from? There was no Temple, no tabernacle, no Levites and here, here is this mystery man Melchizedek. Melchizedek blesses Abram and brings him wine and bread (foreshadowing again to the coming Jesus and his last supper and our celebration of Jesus as the High Priest in the breaking of bread and drinking of wine) The story of Jesus and our redemption is woven throughout the Bible like a masterful tapestry. Abram responds in worship by giving with a grateful heart toward God's priest Mel. This sets up a model of giving out of a heart of gratitude for the blessings God pours out on us. So we respond to God's giving to us in worship, giving to God financially with a deep sense of thankfulness for who God is and what He has done for us.

Take a minute to read about this mysterious Melchizedek found in other places in scripture. Check out Hebrews 7.

Also, is there something big going on in your life you need some serious help with? Like an army of 318 men would be really nice to have get your back with. What about the God of the Cosmoses? Cry out to God to rescue you from whatever it is you are afraid of and He is faithful to deliver.

The Dark Night of the Soul

"That term comes from a sixteenth-century spiritual classic by St. John of the Cross. The book tells how the child of God enters into deeper love and faith by experiencing temporary darkness and seeming separation from God. It is not an easy thing to experience, but sometimes necessary. Abram had three great concerns. During that "dark-night" experience, God met all three of them: his safety, his heirs and his land." Warren Wiersbe

This chapter doesn't stand out as one of Abram's greatest, but God always does his part. God begins by comforting and telling him not to fear. I don't know about you, but there are times when life is a bit overwhelming and it is comforting to remember these words God spoke to Abram here "Don't be afraid, I will protect you." These reassurances of God's protecting us are found all through the Bible and the sad truth is that you and I also respond to God like Abram in doubt and uncertainty.

But God is resilient and he knows when we are a little unsure and we need a little reassurance. It isn't that we have abandoned our faith; we know our help is coming and when we rest in His promises then our faith will be counted as righteousness.

When have you doubted God?

Why is it sometimes hard to trust God and His timing in our lives?

What area of your life do you find it hard to trust God?

Will you ask Him to help you trust Him?

Walk Like an Egyptian

Let's be honest, this isn't one of Abram and Sarai's greatest moments. God had made a promise to Abram and Sarai to give them children, so many descendants they will be more than the stars 15:6 and yet they grew tired of waiting on God and they took matters into their own hands. Sarai suggests Abram sleep with Hagar and Abram takes her as a second wife. Of course, this back fires on Abram and she blames him later, but that's another movie called "He said she said." Our focus is what was God up to in all of this? Doing what He does best Verse 7. In all of this dysfunction and trying to take matters into their own hands and making babies with Hagar, Abram & Sarai got things all muddled up.

God goes to Hagar, an Egyptian not an Israelite, and does what He does best, loves the disenchanted. If Abram would have waited on the Sovereign God to fulfill the promise and not gone on his own to have "relations" with that woman things could have been better. So God promises to bless Hagar as she is mixed up in all this and her response is awesome! She calls God a new name we haven't seen yet. Beer-lahai-roi which means, "You are the God who sees me" which is the premise behind our journey together. God sees everything, hears every cry we weep, every laugh we giggle and is constantly pursuing us.

Have you been tempted to take ungodly steps to achieve a godly goal?

Does that really justify your actions or should you wait on God?

Deal or No Deal 17

Genesis 17 starts out awesome! I love the way God slowly reveals himself to his people over time. We just learned in the last chapter a new name that reveals the character of God and here we get another one. God tells Abram "I Am El-Shaddai" which means God Almighty. God reveals gently without the fan fair of great acts or signs and wonders. He doesn't need any of that because Abram has seen God's faithful blessing and God says I Am bigger and more powerful than you can ever imagine, and yet, I care deeply for you and the people I love.

Genesis 17 again is one of those chapters that makes me laugh. Don't take this the wrong way but God has given me a funny sense of humor and looking at life my observations on Ch 17 may offend some of you. I'm sorry; I don't try to write shocking things for controversy, I just call 'em as I see 'em.

Oh yeah and if you are a girl you might want to FFWD to the end of the Chapter. By the way, the sign of the covenant here for guys covered the whole household.

So back to our story already in progress. We find young Abe @ 99 chatting with God and God is laying out His plan of a covenant between God and His chosen people. God asks Abram to do his part and live a blameless life and serve God faithfully and in return, God will bless Abram and his family with countless descendants. This deal is pretty good. Not only will God give Abram many descendants, God goes on in verse4 to say you will be the father of many nations! This deal is getting better all the time! You will have kings in your lineage and I'm changing your name to Abraham to fit this profound change for a young 99-year-old guy who is going to be the father of many nations.

Verse 7 is overwhelming! "I will **always** be your God." God knew the rocky road ahead; He knew the deceit and betrayal of his people. The adulterous hearts and stubborn denial of mankind all the way to the cross and yet God still says, "I will **always** be your God and the God of your descendants." How great is our God? Sing with me. How great **is** our God and all will see **How Great** is **our** God!

This deal/covenant so far is a pretty good deal and I'm sure Abraham is all in right up until verse 11. This is where you hear the tires screech as he slams on the brakes and you hear Abraham saying Whoa wait a minute, you want me to do WHAT? Why?! Why that? Why down there?? Can't you just teach me a sweet secret handshake or gang sign I can flash so people will know I am part of this covenant with you God. And another thing, nobody will even be able to see it and know I'm yours! How about a sweet neck tattoo that when people see it, they say "Whoa, that guy belongs to the Almighty God we better respect and fear him cause he's connected."

But no. "Seriously?? You want me to cut my . . . you know, as a sign of my agreeing to the deal?!" Ok, we know Abraham loved God deeply and God loved Abraham. But to breeze over the details, the fine print of this contract is to be amiss my friend! No guy in the history of man's existence wants to be cut "down there." Why would God choose such an odd sign of this covenant? My answer is one that is so obvious and yet I think profound. So much so, I've never heard or read anyone else brave enough in any commentary or footnote to mention it. (Which could just mean I'm way off, but I don't think so.)

What I'm about to say isn't meant as a joke or crude. It's just my unique perspective on seeing God's interaction with us. I think one of the reasons God put the sign of the covenant "down there" for Abraham and all the men after is because that is a place we would see it **every day.** Many times a day in fact. I also think that down the road David could have avoided his adultery if he would have paid more attention to the sign of the covenant. The same goes for every guy throughout history, including you. If we were about to commit adultery or have sex outside the bonds of marriage, and we looked down and saw a neon sign "down there" that said "Whoa wait a minute! Remember our deal? Serve me faithfully and live blamelessly." I think we would stop a lot of our sin right there.

And what if guys, every time from now on when you go #1 you remember, Hey, I'm supposed to serve God today, I'm supposed to live a blameless life. Am I doing that since the last time I saw the reminder of the sign of the covenant? (Like 2 hrs ago) I also think humans are forgetful, fickle creatures. Throughout scripture, there are these constant themes of God saying remember what happened here, put a pile of rocks or write it down or have a party every year or do this in remembrance of me. But time and time again, we just forget. Moses goes up the mountain to be with God and the people forget and quickly turn to worship false gods. Jesus tells Peter he will deny him and Peter says no way! Within 12 hours Peter says "Je-who?? Never heard of the guy" 3 times and when the rooster crows Peter says "Doh, how could I forget!" We need a constant reminder that we are God's and He is ours.

So say what you want, but I think the sign of the covenant was put where it was as a constant reminder for us forgetful guys.

Welcome back to the ladies who may have skipped that last part. Verse 15-18 Sarah is now brought in as part of God's plan of redemption and despite Abraham being a pillar of faith, he lost it here. And I understand Abraham's laughing. God has a funny sense of humor sometimes and so when God revealed the details to the young honeymooners at 90 &100 years old Abraham couldn't help but laugh. I mean wouldn't you! This is farther removed from Adam and the life expectancy was dropping. Abraham lived to 175, but still at this point, he was an old dude! Think of the oldest couple you know—90 something—cruising around in their hove-around scooters and they are going to have a baby!

I love the absurdity of this story! The Bible is filled with things that are too absurd to be made up. There are too many details of honest reactions and real life that gives scripture the aroma of integrity. If God would have made this promise to Abe and Sara when they were in their 20's big deal! So the only way a 90 &100 year old are having a stork sign put in front of their tent with "it's a boy" on it is by the power of the Almighty God.

Because of Jesus, the sign of the covenant with Abraham is no longer required, but what is? Check out Galatians 5:6 for the answer for guys and girls.

18 It's A Boy!

When Sarah hears God's plan her response is the same, she cracks up! So God replies "Why are you laughing?" And she says "What? I wasn't laughing." And they're is a kind of comical back and forth between Sarah and God over her honest response and her trying to cover it up.

I'm not a woman, so I have no idea what is like to want to have a baby but can't. I have friends that are married and can't have a child and they desperately want one. I've seen the longing and heartache, tears, and waves of questions and emotions. Why God? Now multiply what we know times some big number and I think you begin to get a glimpse of Sarah's pain. Our society is kind and compassionate toward woman who can't have a baby. (Yes, I know it's sometimes the guys fault) But imagine if you were shamed at work or church and in your neighborhood and on Facebook for being barren.

Sarah lived with that for 90 years and by this point in her life, I'm sure she had long come to terms with the fact she would never have a child of her own. So in disappointment and probably shame she let her husband take on Hagar as a wife to provide him a child to carry on his name. The hurt and pain that Sarah felt is palatable from chapter 16-18. So when God says to this 90 year old woman "You're gonna have a baby" it's understandable that she laughed.

But God wasn't laughing and He says to her, I remember you, I love you Sarah and I haven't abandoned you and I'm going to bless your sandals off! This entire birth announcement and the following 9 months and the arrival of wittle Isaac happened in such a way that only God could get the glory. So she chuckles a little here, but when Isaac finally arrived and that chuckle of disbelief turns to full on laughter of overwhelming joy.

Look at the world around you; do you think we have become numb to the evil around us?

How does our society desensitize people to sinful behavior?

What is something you have thought was impossible for God to do? Ask God to give you faith to believe like Sarah in the unbelievable that only God can accomplish.

Fire From Above

    I have always been disturbed by this chapter in the bible! Why would Lot throw out his 2 virgin daughters!? Is it because he knew the men were homosexual and wouldn't hurt them? Or was it to show the depth of the depravity of Sodom and the depravity of Lot? Then we see the intervention of the angels and the ensuing Armageddon is right from a Hollywood apocalyptic movie. Angles grabbing people by the hand running as explosions rain down from the sky, cars and gas stations blowing up . . . oh wait, camels and camel depots exploding as everyone runs in super slow motion as shrapnel flies past their heads in 3-D!

    Verse 28 reminds me of the scene in Star Wars IV when Luke returns home to find his home and aunt and uncle burned and smoke billowing. That is what Abraham saw when he got up the next morning you can hear the Star Wars song *Burning homestead* lightly playing in the background.

    God couldn't find 50,40,30,20 or even 10 righteous people there and as an act of mercy and kindness, God spared lot. Then chapter 19 ends with drunken incest which results in the Moabites and Ammonites who later become enemies of Israel. Like I said, this is one messed up chapter!

Look around your world today. Would God have a hard time finding 50, 40, 30 or even 10 truly godly people around you? How can it be tough to lead a Godly life in a sinful society? What specific steps do you need to take this week to avoid temptation?

Liar Liar Pants on Fire!

As this story unfolds in verse 3 God's first words to Abimelech are "You're a Dead Man" spoken like a true father who finds a guy trying to sleep with his daughter! But whoa, wait a minute. Why was this guy trying to sleep with Sarah? Wasn't Sarah in her 90's! She must have been one hot 90-year-old lady! And another thing, why was Abraham lying?! . . . **again** like he did to Pharaoh in 12:13 and he's gonna do it again in chapter 26 (spoiler Alert) When I ask the question I don't mean <u>why</u> I know why, verse 11, but **why** in that I thought Abraham was supposed to be this holy blameless man of God.

Do you smell it? The answer is in the aroma of authenticity of scripture. If I ever write my life story, I'm going to be handsome, the strongest man around with ripped abs, teeth that sparkle in the sun light. I'm James Bond on the weekdays and Batman on the weekends. I will be a blameless hero loved and adored by my wife and children as I flawlessly lead them. (Just check out my bio at the back of the book.) But that's not the story of Abraham, or anyone else in scripture except Jesus. Just when you get to know a guy in scripture and you hear of the intimacy they have with God you think "Wow this guy is amazing he must glow of his holiness everywhere he goes." Then you are reminded of James 5:17 "Elijah was a human as we are."

The Bible is the real life story of real men and women struggling with everyday life. Sometimes their faith and hope in God is blindingly radiant and sometimes you have to give them an ESPN "Come on Man! What were you thinking?" And yet through it, all God's love is unwavering despite Abraham's lack of faith, cowardice and deceitfulness God still protected Sarah.

But wait, there's more! The story ends with a twist. Abraham and Sarah are given a bunch of $$ and Land, which is nice, but the real kicker is what happens to Abimelech and his family in verse 17.

God blesses Abimelech and his family with fertility because of his faithfulness and fear of the Lord. What a wonderful and gracious God we have to pour out his love and blessing freely.

How has God been gracious to you?

How do you deal with the consequences of bad decisions you've made in the past?

Promises Promises

This chapter is sandwiched in promises. Promises are fulfilled, broken, past lies are remembered and the chapter ends on a promise. I promise you, it's a good one. God's promise to Sarah and Abraham is fulfilled with the arrival of little Isaac. His arrival comes with much joy and Sarah's chuckles from the first news have grown into laughter. You can see the smile on her face as she exclaims "God has brought me laughter." But with the arrival of Isaac and the great Joy there also came increased strife between Sarah and Hagar. You can feel the tension that had been building up for years and the resentment coming to a head. Until finally Sarah snapped and demanded that Hagar and Ishmael be cast out.

So the fix Sarah thought she had found for their infertility problem back in chapter 16 only brought strife and heartache. Abraham packed them up and sent them on their way and as Hagar wondered around she had to remember Beer-lahai-roi = you are the God who sees me. Despite the broken promises from Sarah and Abraham to Hagar, God is faithful to His promises. He provides water and nourishment for Ishmael as he grew up in Paran.

Verse 23 we see Abimelech return and he sees the evidence that God is defiantly blessing Abraham and Abimelech wants to make a treaty. But there is a problem, Abraham has lied in the past and his credibility is shot. The broken promise Abraham made to Abimelech when they first met about Sarah being his sister is still fresh in his mind. So he makes Abraham swear to him with God as the witness and the one to hold Abraham accountable if he lies again.

In the words of the great philosophers Naked Eyes "Promises Promises you knew you'd never keep." That was Abimelech's fear dealing with Abraham and being a man of his word.

Lying is easy and profitable. It temporarily gets you out of trouble and can help you get what you want in the short term. But when you get caught, your creditability is shot! No matter what you say, the person will be questioning whether you are telling the truth or another clever lie. Abraham was facing the consequence of his lie to Abimelech and the same is true for you and me. If you lie to your parents or friends eventually, you're going to get caught and when you do, it will take a long time to earn their trust again. Take a minute to examine your pattern of lies. Do you lie about stupid things or maybe you're covering up big things. It doesn't matter, as a Christian you are called to a life of integrity. Integrity is doing what is right even when no one is looking. This short chapter is a reminder of the fickle and deceitful heart of man and at the same time, it amplifies the everlasting consistency of God being faithful to His promises.

What about you? Are you a man/woman of your word? Do you lie when you get put on the spot? Do you lie when you are afraid of getting caught doing something you're not supposed to be doing? Or lie to cover up not doing something you were supposed to be doing? Or lie to make yourself look better or lie to tell the person what you think they want to hear? Are you a person of Integrity when no one is looking? Take a second to confess any lies you may be living to God and ask Him to help you resist the temptation to live a life of lying.

Domo Arigato Mr. Roboto

This chapter begins with God calling his beloved Abraham and Abraham responding as he always did "Here I am Lord." I wish I was always that responsive to God's calling. A lot of times I'm more like Gideon or Moses, "Are you sure you mean me Lord, I think you got the wrong number," or we just don't answer "We're sorry the party you are trying to reach is not available please try your **call** again later."

I love working in the yard. It's quiet and peaceful and gives me time to pray and think. I wonder what was going through Abrahams mind as he was chopping wood the next morning after God had told him to sacrifice his boy Isaac. I think we make the mistake of thinking Abraham was some giant Faith Robot. We think that Abraham always said in a robotic way "Yes Lord that computes." "I will obey." But I think as he swung that axe chopping the wood to burn his son, his heart had to be conflicted. He probably welled up with tears as he was providing the fuel to cook his little boy that he loved deeply.

Verse 5 Abraham tells his servant that "we" will be right back. Does Abraham think God was joking or lying when he said "Go and sacrifice Isaac whom you love so much"? Or was Abraham's statement one of nervous faith? "We will be right back; everything's going to be okay. There's no way my God would really do that. He loves me, and I love Him and He knows how much I love Isaac. He will provide another way. I really don't know what's going on here God, but I love you and I trust you. So I will listen and follow you where ever you lead me."

There is a great song by the band Siler's Bald called *Getting Back*. At the end of the song, there is this great chorus that says "today I will follow wherever you lead me, seek your perfection in all that I do." Read that line 3 times over and over. They chant this line and that resonates from the pages of scripture here in Genesis as the heart of Abraham faithfully cries out to God.

RANDOM THOUGHT

Abraham's nephews were named Uz and Buz! That is awesome! They had to be the first linebackers with crew cuts or Buz at least had to have a space suit. Because his families descendants would go "to infinity and beyond" Ahahahahah Come on man that's funny! 'Cause his name is Buz and his niece Rebekah marries Isaac and God blessing them with so many descendants, more than the **stars** and in that lineage is Mary, Jesus' mommy. And Jesus is the infinite creator of the universe and his rule goes from "infinity and beyond". Now it's funny right! :)

THGUOHT MODNAR

What about you? Can you say that from your heart? Here I am Lord. Do you live that out? Everyday waking up saying "Ok Lord, I'm not sure what is coming my way today, but I will follow wherever you lead me today."

Dearly Beloved . . . 23

We see Sarah dies here at the age of 127 and Abraham morns the loss of his soul mate Sarah. Abraham had lived his faith out loud in his community of foreigners in such a way that they counted him a "friend" and "honored prince" what a testimony to his integrity!

Not to sound morbid, but this chapter is a good reminder of our mortality. Somebody once said "None of us are getting out of here alive. One day they will paint you up like a clown, and put you in the ground!" So when it comes time for you to go home, what will people say about the life you lived?

Lego Death Star & God's Sovereignty

Chapter 24 opens with what I can only imagine was the first handshake. It has evolved over the years from placing your hand under a guy's thigh to the sweet roman one where you grab the forearm to today's standard handshake. (Notable mention to the 80's invention of the chain link handshakes of grabbing the thumb to the fingertips to the thumb spin snap. Which I often performed in my parachute pants days as a greeting or to complete an oath or transaction of a star wars figure.) Needless to say, I'm glad this one progressed away from the thigh thingy, 'cause that's pretty gross.

And while I'm distracted by cultural differences, I had to do a double take and read verse 22 twice. "A gold ring for her nose." This wasn't a tiny nose stud, but a ring and matching bracelets! I hope it was a small one to go through one side of the nostril and not a big one through the middle like a bull. Cause again, that's kinda gross and hard to kiss a girl if that's where she had it. But I digress.

I love reading God's word! I love seeing the little pieces of the puzzle begin to fit together. When you look at the Bible as God's complete story of our creation and God's calling/pursuing us all the way to the completed work on the cross. It is kinda like getting a 1000 piece puzzle. But for you and me, we have the whole thing completed, we know God's story of redemption that is revealed from Genesis to Revelations. It's not like we have a pile of 1000 pieces and no box cover to know what it looks like. It's not even that we have the pieces and the box cover and we have to find the pieces and try figure out where they all go. I'm speaking metaphorically about our lives specifically and the bigger picture of theology and God's sovereignty. Some people who do not know God in an intimate loving relationship will say things like "The Bible is just mans way of trying to explain things so they make up a god etc, etc." So when they look at their life and the world around them all they see are puzzle pieces with no box.

But that is Ludicrous! It's 2011 and we are living in the "modern age" yet we are clueless on the origin of our planet and humans and platypus' and love. Without God, life is just a Bazillion piece puzzle and we are scrounging around trying to figure out on our own where does this piece fit? And is that a tree with a piece of cloud on it or water with a baby monkey on a pigs back?? We are clueless to the Big Picture of the existence of the universe and even more clueless to the question of "Why am I here??" "Am I living just to breath? Am I truly living or am I just breathing to death?"*(The Bravery & Lecrae)

The Bible is God's story of his plan of intimate love for His people that he is pursuing. I'm going to switch analogies here on you and I may lose some of you, but flip to the end of this chapter real quick for those of you who have never built LEGOS®. This is the LEGO® Death Star it has 3803 piece and cost $400 and I believe it is a better analogy than the puzzle one. Because with a puzzle you get a box with a picture of what you are to build and then you dump it out, strain and search for image recognition and try to shove some pieces in and hope they fit and hope you don't lose a piece or your dog doesn't come by and eat one!

That is not a good analogy of God's word and his Big Picture purpose for our existence, but the LEGO® Death Star is. (Don't worry; I'm getting to Gen 24, just hang with me. Oh and don't take the analogy of the death star itself too far as a weapon of mass destruction from an evil empire, I just used it because I'm a geek and would love to build a 3,803 piece LEGO® set. (by the way if you want to get me one for my birthday I would love it!) The analogy is still there if you use a LEGO® Empire State building or whatever, so don't get lost here :))

Now imagine I came up to you and gave you this completed Death Star already built and the instruction manual. That is what God has done with His Word. The Bible is the instruction manual and his completed work is our redemption. The Bible is incapable of error and pivotal for the foundational integrity of Christianity. If the Bible is not the 100% Word of God, then everything implodes on itself. Remember, this is God's story, He is telling us about Himself through the Bible.

I also believe the LEGO® set is a good analogy in the area of science and discovery of our world. As humans, we come across something in space or human bodies or animals and we say "wow we've discovered *X*." And we now know that the reason say a Platypus flies south to Orlando for the winter is because of an internal glad that salivates this time of year for the taste of theme park churros, etc, etc. All we are doing is finding all the little steps God used to build X. X = humans or space exploration or whatever. God is the designer/Creator and as we study life and science around us, all we are doing is discovering how God built whatever!

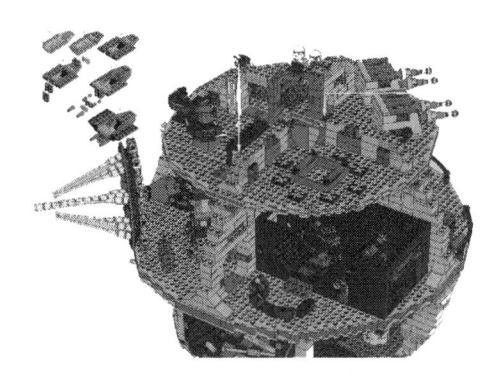

In Genesis 24 Abraham is adamant that his servant follow the instructions that God had given him to stay in that area because God's big picture plan was to call Abraham (add LEGO® Brick) bless Sarah with baby (add brick) build the nation of Israel (add bricks). You and I have the completed intricate story of how God's plan of redemption unfolded one piece at a time. We can see the completed work and the instruction manual and know God is Sovereign and pursuing us because He loves us.

Do you believe God has a plan for your life?

What are some ways you have seen God's plan for your life unfolding brick by brick?

The Perfect Family

Abraham was a strong man, not because he could do a lot of pushups, but because at age 140 he got remarried and had 6 more kids! That is impressive! Abraham finally goes home to be with his family in heaven verse 8. But Verse 9 has something interesting that you may breeze right over. Look who was there to bury Abraham. Isaac **and** Ishmael! Ishmael who had been cast out by Sarah and now he comes back for what I can only imagine is an awkward funeral with family against family. Ishmael was the first born and got nothing in inheritance and Isaac received everything.

Despite the hurt feelings, jealousy, and anger Ishmael may have felt, God blessed Ishmaels' family. But the hatred, resentment, and division in families can be devastating and Ishmael's descendants "lived in open hostility toward all their relatives." I'm sure your family is the perfect family like the Cleavers. But I have seen the smallest things rip a family apart. Brother against brother and sister and then they bring their kids in on the mess.

This chapter kind of reminds me of when you get a bad cut on your hand (Ishmael being cast our and it hurt deep and bled, but in time healed to a scab) Then you're walking by a piece of fabric grabs it and off it comes and opens the wound again. Sorry for that graphic analogy, but this chapter started out with new love and life and shifted to solemn closure to Abraham's "ripe old age" but then something gets picked and we have this shift to dysfunctional families with Isaac and Ishmael. And it only gets worse with the arrival of Jacob and Esau. Again, if I'm writing the history of my family, we are the perfect family. I clean up my story to be the perfect husband and father. Scripture has the pungent odor of real life that gives it its authenticity and not a flowery fable.

I love verse 21 and the intimacy with God that Isaac had learned from his father Abraham. He pleads in prayer on behalf of his wife and God is faithful to his promise to Abraham and his descendants and blesses Rebekah with 2 children.

Now the story of Esau and Jacob's birth always cracks me up! First I have this image of little furry Esau (Like the baby Grinch) and Jacob with his hand on Esau's heel as they go out! I bet Rebekah was so glad to finally give birth to those two so they could take their fight outside as mom's say. When my wife was pregnant with our 1st daughter, toward 7 months I remember seeing a foot pushing on her belly (which always freaked me out). But Jacob and Esau were probably cage fighting in the womb and giving Rebekah a fit.

We aren't told the age of Jacob and Esau when the transaction of the birthright gumbo took place, but I'm going to do a little Crime Scene Investigation and say they were high school age around 16 years old. I say that based on three things: 1. Verse 27 begins by referring to them as boys grownup not men and 2. By their appetite: I have witnessed high school guys devour 6 pizzas in 30 seconds like a swarm of locus! So Esau, in his mind was starving to death. 3. The finally clue is most teens have no regard for the future. It's too far away. Esau's disdain for his receiving what his father was going to leave him was so far out in the future; he didn't really care about that stuff now. The text says Esau had "contempt for his birthright." He wasn't worried about it he just wanted a taco! But in Esau's haste and Jacobs wisdom God placed another brick in its place.

In all fairness here, Ishmael and Isaac had some pretty big problems that started the divide, but what about your family? Are there some little things brewing that need to be dealt with in love and forgiveness before your whole family is torn apart and your kids and grandkids are living in "open hostility toward each other?"

Trick or Treat

Isaac wasn't born yet when his daddy pulled this same trick on Abimelech, but Abraham must have shared stories with his son. Here we see Isaac and his beautiful wife try the same trick. "She's my sister." I'm going to try that from now on when I introduce my wife to people. It's fun to see the flower of God's promises unfold on the pages of scripture. From Abraham to Isaac, Isaac to his messed up boys & his dysfunctional family, God is still faithful despite our fallen condition.

Verse 24 we see God gently reveal himself to Isaac as his father's God and Isaac's grandfather's God. What a great story to have! Some Christians I meet who have grown up in the church feel like they "have no story." They were never involved in drugs or partying or selling children and kittens on EBay as they rebelled from their parents and God.

But I think they've got it all wrong and backwards. People like Isaac and those of you today that grew up in the church with parents and grandparents that love the Lord have the MOST AMAZING STORY! I am jealous of their story! My heart yearns to know what it would have been like growing up with a father who loved Christ with reckless abandon. And so for some of you the response for a Godly heritage story should propel you to worship just like Isaac did. And those of you who maybe don't have that example, it should propel you to make certain your kids will be able to say that when they grow up.

What Godly legacy have your parents or grandparents modeled for you? Take a minute to just tell them thanks.

Ask God to grow you into a Godly man or woman so that you can leave a Godly legacy behind.

27
Liar Liar los pantalones en el fuego

As Godly a man Isaac may have been, his family was still a mess. Isaac lied about Rebekah being his sister and this chapter is full of lies and deceit, conniving, favoritism, blessing, devastation, disappointment and rage. That's more than most reality TV shows can pack in one season let alone 1 chapter of the Bible about a patriarch Godly family!

The conniving begins when Rebekah eavesdrops on a conversation between Isaac and Esau. Talk about a "house divided." And this isn't just 2 rival college football teams. The bumper sticker on the back of their donkey wouldn't just be a split down the middle it's more like mom loves Jacob and dad loves Esau and there is no hiding it.

I'm not sure why this happens in families, but it does. I've seen it. You've seen it, where one parent or parents seem to favor one kid over the other. The resulting pain and separation that comes from this are devastating and long lasting. The sad thing is the kids are the victims of the parents messed up approach to parenting.

When we had our first daughter Kaleigh, we were overwhelmed with love we had never known before for our baby girl. She was amazing and fun and cuddly and loveable. So when we found out my wife was pregnant again we were overjoyed, but also a tad apprehensive. I remember having a conversation with my wife as we both had run into an unexpected fear. Could we really love another child as much as our first? We loved her so much we were afraid the youngest would be left out.

That's the funny thing about new parents, they are so young and dumb :) When Mary Ashleigh was born, we were overwhelmed again as this tidal wave of deeper joy and love flowed for both girls. From day one, we have been intentional to build our girls up in their uniqueness and love them and treat them the same. I credit my wife for always working with our girls to love each other and build each other up. Again, I don't share this with you to say "look at us, we figured it out, we're great." I only share it because I've seen the division that can creep into a family and drive a deep wedge if we are not careful to love our kids equally and built them up together.

So momma bear plots to deceive poppa bear Isaac. And the dominoes begin to fall. I wish I could have seen Jacob with the goat hair all over his arms and neck because that is a funny looking Facebook profile picture.

The lies begin to flow in verse 19 when Jacob claims to be Esau and he is caught off guard when he is asked how he found the kill so quickly. Like we said before, it's easy to lie and one lie usually leads to about 6 others to sustain it. Esau being quick on his thinking says "uhh God gave it to me." Now I'm not sure why God doesn't step in here and smite Jacob. Because everyone knows that song kids sing "liars go to Hell, liars go to Hell." And what about the whole "You better step back God's about to fry this dude with a bolt of lightning?" I searched the Bible for the evidence to support those jolly kids' songs & countless stories of people being fried and liars being shot straight to H-E-double hockey sticks, but I couldn't find them.

So is it okay to lie? Abraham did it, Isaac did it and here we have Jacob whose name today means deceiver. The answer is no. God is pretty clear on this that we are not to give false statements against our neighbors and that Satan is the father of lies. God is not passive here nor is he quick to "smite". If he was, we would have all been wiped out long ago.

Verse 27 Jacob had sealed the deal by using Esau's Manly Musk Old Spice and Jacob receives the blessing that belonged to Esau. Now technically Esau already sold Jacob his birthright for the squirrel gumbo, so it technically wasn't stealing and deceit on Rebekah and Jacob's part it was fulfilling an oath between the 2 brothers. The dad and Esau didn't really want it to turn out God's way. "God chose Jacob in the womb." Romans 9 tells us, but God's plans will not be thwarted by man.

Did they lie and deceive Isaac? Yes, but it was to obtain what was rightfully Jacobs now because of Esau selling his birthright.

RANDOM THOUGHT

Verse 28-29 I like to use these verses when someone sneezes. It's just fun instead of just saying "God bless you" you actually give them a blessing from the Bible. I like to mix it up and say "May God give you many goats & children and may your family live long and prosper."

THGUOHT MODNAR

What sinful behavior do you tend to rationalize? Who can you ask to hold you accountable when you're tempted to rationalize? What is something specific you can do to ease the friction between you and a family member?

Kissing Cousins & Led Zeppelin

Jacob's departs from his family out of self-preservation so he travels over the Euphrates and through the woods to uncle's house he goes to find a wife. So he goes to uncle Laban on his mother's side of the family to find a cousin to kiss.

Meanwhile back at the Hall of Justice, Esau scrambles to make dad proud by visiting his uncle Ishmael and marry one of his cousins. Now I know you may be confused here. I know what you're thinking "wait; there's a Padd-aram, Tennessee??" Because TN is one of the few places, you can marry your 1st cousin. No, it's not in Tennessee and no, I'm not making that up, you can look it up, it's still legal! Now it may seem odd or gross in our culture, but considering the pagan alternatives for a Godly family, it was their best option.

Jacob unintentionally inspires Led Zeppelin's most popular song that is banned from most guitar stores. Unfortunately, Led Zep only picked up on the stairway to heaven and missed the best part of God's promise to Jacob that He is the God of Jacob's father and his father's father and that the pursuit is still on. This isn't the story of Jacob going out into the wilderness to find God or build some alter and sacrifice things and search for the meaning of life. Jacob was simply resting for the night on his Tempur-Pedic rock and God comes to him and says "I love you; I always have and always will. I will bless you and your family and protect you and give you some sweet real estate."

Bethel, what a great place! There are about 5 million churches and camps with the name Bethel in their title of every flavor of denomination. But this Ebenezer built by Jacob in the small town of Luz (I bet they had a DQ, it just sounds like a town with a DQ) this town is transformed into a great memorial of Jacobs encounter with the living God.

I gotta say, I'm not a fan of English. The class in high school, not the language or people group. I'm also not particularly impressed with Jacob's use of the conditional sentence structure in his response to God's flipping sweet revelation. (Ok, for the record I had to look up the term "conditional sentence" but I remembered it from science or English or P.E. or somewhere that it's that If-then clause) So Jacob says "IF you will do this for me God, THEN I will like you."

We baulk @ Jacob's conditional sentence to the Almighty God of the universe, but wait a minute, let's be honest . . . haven't you ever done that? "God IF you will only _____ THEN I swear I'll _____ forever and ever Amen." I know when I was young in my faith I did that, as if I was bringing something magnificent to the barging table with God. Now my prayers have evolved to "Come on God, let me win the lotto and I'll give you a few $ for some missionaries or a sweet multimillion dollar youth room/theme park with a Taco Bell Baja Mountain Dew waterfall built in."

As long as our faith resides in the conditional sentence phase, we are on a stationary bike peddling faster and faster getting nowhere! We have to make that transition in our faith to drop the IF-Then clause to a "I trust you regardless of my circumstances and today I will follow where ever you lead me because you are my God."

Will you commit to do that right now? If so, tell God.

Love, Facespace and Princess Leah

Long before dating websites where people went to find their soul mates, there was The Well. The well seemed to be a great place to meet new people and the girl/man of your dreams/destiny aka sovereign plan of God. Isaac met Rebekah at a spring getting water (24:15), well technically it was Abraham's unnamed servant who went to the water and met Rebekah for Abraham. For Jacob it was at the watering hole as they say out west where he met the girl of his dreams Rachel. Hagar met God at a well in 16:14 and named the well "The well of the living one who sees me." Which, my brain immediately FFWD's to another woman at a well who met a man in John 4 the "woman at the well." We never get her name, but we know that the living water found in Jesus quenches the deepest thirst.

If you do a brief study of wells in scripture (like I just did for fun), you see they were the Facespace/match.com of their time. It was a central place to meet new people, share life, make oaths, be betrayed by big fat meanies etc. Which actually transitions us to what's ahead for poor Jacob.

RANDOM THOUGHT

VERSE 9 tells us that Rachel was a shepherd. Is there a female word for a girl shepherd? Like mailman just sounds better than mail woman (no offense if you are a mail person) I like the term Shepherdess. So from here on anytime we come across another woman who is a sheep watcher we will call them shepherdess's cause it just sounds more effeminate kinda like Princess. Ok, something funny just happened. I just made that term up and my spell checker didn't see anything wrong with shepherdess. Which I thought was strange and a quick Google search revealed I didn't in fact make up the word I just thought I made up, it has already existed. I'm smarter than I meant to be! Talk about a **random thought** inside a random thought!

THGUOHT MODNAR

Jacob meets the gal of his dreams verse 1 and he kisses her on the first date! (I'm kidding; it was just a friendly greeting) And then he wept. I'm going to assume his weeping was out of an overwhelming joy from a long journey following God's plan for his life from Beersheba to Haran to culminate in a providential encounter with his beautiful new bride to be. And not because he was searching the world over thinking he would find true love and he finally meets his cousin whom he is to marry and she is so ugly and buck toothed that she could "eat corn through a picket fence." (Hee Haw Song)

No, the truth is the first one of course, true love plus a tangible feeling of God working out His plan and promise is overwhelming and will cause any man to cry. On to match.com, what a great love story between Jacob and Rachel! She was so beautiful (verse 17) that he was willing to work 7 years to have her hand in marriage! That's true love my friend, look at verse 20, 7 years only seemed like a few days. I'm sure Jacob's conversation with Rachel went something like this: "I know we've only know each other 4 weeks and 3 days, but to me it seems like 9 weeks and 5 days. The 1st day seemed like a week & the 2nd day seemed like 5 days, and the 3rd day seemed like a week again & the 4th day seemed like 8 days. And the 5th day you went to see your mother and that seemed just like a day, and then you came back and later on the 6th day . . ." (Navin R Johnson)

So this dream comes true of love at first sight at the well and 7 years of working and waiting finally comes to an end with a beautiful wedding. Everyone is invited, they bring in the cake boss of their time, and he makes an amazing cake. Jacob and Rachel "were as close together as a bride and groom, they ate the food, they drank the wine, everybody was having a good time except . . ." (U2—Until the End of the World) Laban.

Laban was a dirty lying, conniving Jerk! I'm sorry, he just makes me angry. Jacob was a hard working honest young guy who never lied or deceived anyone he . . . oh wait. Yeah this family is full of trickery so Jacob should have been a little more on his guard, but love is blind. Literally, in Jacobs case as we will see!

For me, my wife had an uncle who messed with my head. He told me a few weeks before our wedding that they had a tradition in their family of snatching the groom after the ceremony sometime and tying him up in a van and keeping them from their wedding night festivities as a prank! I didn't know this guy; I couldn't tell if he was messing with me or what. All I knew was I waited 4 long years and I couldn't wait to be with my new bride. So I was in constant suspicion and in fear that whole afternoon after I said "I do." Taking pictures, the reception . . . when was he coming for me?! As silly as that sounds it pales in comparison to the trick Laban pulled here on Jacob. And no, that sucka never got a hold of me, I kept my eyes WIDE open and had friends watching Uncle's every move and then I bolted for the car and away we fled.

Verse 23 I don't know if it was super dark out and maybe there was no moon out, or maybe she had a veil on or maybe Jacob had too much wine to not notice the girl he was sleeping with WASN'T RACHEL! How do you not notice these tiny details?!? Whatever the case, the next morning had to be shocking for Jacob verse25

He thought he had finally won the beauty of his dreams only to wake up to the older sister! That had to be super awkward. Jacob had to have feelings of hatred toward Laban his now father-in-law for deceiving him. Rachel had to be heartbroken and must have had some resentment toward her sister and father for doing this. I guess the only one happy in the deal was Laban and Leah since they couldn't marry her off to anyone else, now she had a man. And you thought your thanksgiving reunion was awkward!

Jacob has to wait a week and then he gets Rachel, which was nice of Laban to not make Jacob work another 7 years and at the end get her as his wife verse28. Verse 30 tells us of the deep love he had for Rachel, and the story begins to pick up speed and it's easy to breeze right past verse 31, but don't.

I'm always perplexed when people claim that God is distant and uninterested in the intricate details of our lives. God saw the heartbreak and dejection Leah was feeling and it moved God. Our God loves us deeply and cares for us. I have no idea the deep hurt and anguish you may be going through right now, but be encouraged that the God of the universe knows and cares and He hears your cries of pain.

We don't really know much about Princess Leah (sorry, I had to sneak that in there) but there were some psychological issues going on. There are several reasons polygamy is a bad idea and part of it is the emotional void it can cause. I'm not a psychologist and I don't even play one on TV. I'm not a polygamist so I can't speak from experience here. I'm just a guy who has been married 15+ years and I know it is tough to meet the emotional needs of my 1 wife. Jacob has 2 wives and he obviously isn't able to invest in the emotional needs of both of his wives. We see that in the names of 3 of Leah's sons.

Can you imagine if your mom named you, "I wish my husband would love me" or "I'm unloved, here is another son." That's what Leah did with Reuben, Simeon and Levi. I've seen women who do this and you probably have too. They don't feel loved so they want a baby thinking "at least the baby will love me" or the marriage is going down the toilet and the girl thinks if she just gets pregnant, he'll have to stay and love her. It rarely works that way.

Just in the picking of her baby names, you feel the loneliness and heartache for Leah. You also see her trying to find her identity in the reciprocation of affection from Jacob and producing off spring. This goes on until baby #4, Judah whose name means "now I will praise the Lord."

I'm not sure what happened to Leah to change her heart here. Maybe she gave up trying to find love and affection from Jacob and looked to God alone for that. If that was the case that is great! I try desperately to tell the young girls in my youth ministry and my own daughters to find their love and acceptance from God alone. He is the only one who can deeply meet those needs. And if some guy comes along and says, "Hey I like you/love you/ want to marry you," that's great, but it will never compare to the deep love of the Father.

If we find our identity in the knowledge of God's intimate love for us, then all other love that comes along is a nice side item. If my wife always looked to me to fill all her deep emotional needs, she would be left with a void. There is only so much I can do, and even at my best when I put down my phone, laptop, remote, Xbox controller and give my wife undivided emotional attention, I still can only scratch the surface of her needs. My wife's greatness need, my greatest need, your greatest need is to frolic in the depth of the Father's love for us.

Verse 35 Leah finally seems to get it and praises God alone for Judah. She doesn't seem to be desperately seeking the affection of Jacob and then she stops having babies as if to say she finally understands God's love for her.

What voids in your heart are you trying to fill with stuff other than God?

What about the future is hard for you to entrust to God?

Rock-a-by-baby 30

Somebody needs to give these girls a decent baby name book! Naming your children with revenge names just isn't healthy. And poor Jacob has to keep having "relations" with all these woman to have babies! God promised Jacob back in his stairway to heaven encounter that he would have many descendants 28:14, but I'm sure Jacob had no idea he would be caught up in a baby arms race! Rachel's envy of her sister Leah was consuming her and robbing her of the good, God has planned for her.

Whatever peace and contentment Leah may have found with Judah is now gone once the great baby race began. The sad thing is Jacob and Rachel's story started out so romantic but ended up a disaster.

Take a minute to step back from your busy life. Is there something that has so consumed you that it has robbed you of what God wants for your life?

Is there someone you are envious of? Take some time to deal with that before God and ask Him to take away those feelings and heal your heart.

You are now free to move about the country

As Jacob & Rachel **run** out of the country, they are **chased** by Laban; Rachel steals her dad's set of idols! (Verse 19) I'm not sure if she did this like a child steals a dad's pack of cigarettes to hide them to protect dad. (Which is a **bad** idea by the way) or did she want a set of gods for the road?

As I read through this book, the Bible, God's Holy word about how all his good little people worship Him, I find something shocking and consoling all at once. These were some messed up people! Their marriages and families were a wreck, their personal lives often had potholes in them, and yet despite all that mess, you still see the loving, ever patient ever true God of the universe there. Present and involved in the life of His beloved. Why?! Is He blind? Doesn't He see how messed up we are? Can He see the messed up stuff we have buried in the deep alcoves of our hearts? The messed up answer is **yes**! He does see, and yet while we we're messed up sinners, "He loved us. Oh, how he loves us. Oh."

That is the real story here with Jacob and his lies and deceit. The overwhelming love of God consumes us despite our flaws and sin. Laban, Jacob, Rachel and Leah all belong on Jerry Springer not in the Bible! Some people think the Bible is a pretty pop-up picture book of perfect people, but it isn't. It's a book about a messed up group of people desperately running from the only one who loves us unconditionally. The Pursuit of Man.

I am disturbed by the imperfections and messed up life of this family and yet my comfort comes from them as well. If a loving God would love them, then maybe . . . maybe, no forget maybe, I know He loves me. And I am a messed up joker and God loves me in spite of that. After all, it is the sick that need a Dr. and you and I my friend, are the chief of sinners.

Does it bring you comfort that the people in the Bible were real people with messed up stuff in their lives?

32

UFC 1

Ok, for the record Jacob is a sissy. So far, he has betrayed his brother and then runs away, gets tricked into marring 2 sisters, tricks his father in law and runs away again. And coming back to meet Esau he sends the women and children out in front of him! Come on Man! (Verse 8) As I read this prayer in verse 9-12, it is like a nervous guy pinned down in a movie where bullets are flying and the guy is trying to remind God of the deal they had. I read it really fast like "Oh God, oh Lord you gotta help me!" He is freaking out here, because he knows he did his brother dirty and now it's time to face Esau. Big, hairy, scary Esau. Verse 13-20 are all about Jacob revealing what a coward he is and sending his family and livestock ahead while he sat by the camp fire alone . . . alone . . . and then, he appeared!

UFC # 1 Jacob Vs. Angel. In this corner, we have Jacob 40 years old fighting out of Paddan-Aram and in this corner we have, well, and unnamed Angel who invited Brazilian Jujitsu and Kung Fu! As much of a coward as Jacob had been, he finally manned-up enough to go 5 rounds with the Angel! Jacob would walk with a limp the rest of his life as a reminder of the battle he had with God and as a reminder of who was the victor. God didn't limp away. God's name wasn't changed, but "Jacob wrestled the angel and the angel was overcome." And now he was a new man! Israel.

What do you think God was trying to teach Jacob through this cage fight?

Who ends up winning?

Are you "wrestling" with God over something? Are you winning, losing or are you limping along?

Prepare for Battle! 33

After a rough night cage fighting an angel, Jacob looks up to see Esau coming at him with his army of 400 men and he begins to prepare for battle. Today when someone says "woman and children first," it usually is to save them from peril or at a church lunch. Here we see Jacob put the woman and children first . . . out in front of an angry vengeful brother Esau and army of 400! Then Jacob mounts his horse and rides with determination and trembling anxiety all at once toward the brother he betrayed. (Ok, there is no horse, but if this was a movie, and as soon as Hollywood runs out of remakes from the 80's they will find the great stories in scripture and make a movie. And this scene will demand a slow motion horse ride toward his brother and his 400 men waiting with swords drawn and bows at the ready)

For all we know he could have had his hands in his pockets and walked up to his brother and said "Hey bro, long time no see." But I like the first one better. Verse 4 doesn't read the way either of the brothers probably thought their meeting might take place. 20 years is a long time for Esau to think of how he was betrayed and to plot how he would get his revenge. But even the deepest grudges are no match for a humble and contrite heart. Verse 3 tells us Jacob bows before his brother 7 times, this wasn't for show or Jacob groveling like a coward, it was true remorse and humility before a brother that he had hurt deeply.

The result was an overwhelming healing between the 2 brothers. As they catch up and Jacob introduces his family to his brother, you can feel his relief when Jacob says "what a relief to see your friendly smile."

There is a disarming power that comes when the one you loath to the core begins the conversation with "I'm sorry, will you forgive me." I will never forget the time a man in a Church I was serving at began to stir up trouble and misconceptions about what was going on in the youth program. All these allegations were brought to my boss without even talking with me about any of these issues. So when I found out I was seething with anger toward this guy. A week had gone by and as church was letting out our paths crossed in the stairwell so there was no escape. He greeted me and I replied as cordially as I could all the while seething for the way he had wronged me. He asked me if we could meet and talk, so I agreed. I had gathered facts and supporting ammunition to unload on this guy and let him have it! But our meeting didn't go as expected.

I went to the door and rang the bell. I was like Rambo with dual machine guns in each arm ready to mow this dude down. (Verbally of course) But as this man opened the door, he did something I wasn't expecting. The first words out of his mouth were "Matthew, I'm sorry if I hurt you, can you forgive me." And all at once, the heavy armory I had brought just fell off. I was bewildered and dazed by this man's humble approach. So much so, that it completely disarmed me and there could be healing and forgiveness and restoration.

That's what we see with Jacob bowing before the brother he had wronged and the forgiveness and healing that followed. I implore you to do the same. Go to whomever you may have wronged or been wronged by and begin the conversation "_____ can you forgive me for how I hurt you."

Now I know some of you are saying "I didn't do anything, they need to come to me groveling!" And maybe they do, but chances are you've done something whether real or perceived that has hurt them too. So even if you think you're 99.9% in the right, go to that person, and ask them to forgive you for any hurt you may have caused. Then watch how God can open up the floodgates of forgiveness and heal that broken relationship.

So Jacob leaves his brother and stays in a town he didn't really care for. This town Succoth, ha get it? (I'm sorry I spend way too much time with middle and high school guys!) When Jacob finally arrives in Shechem he sets his priorities and builds an alter to worship the God he loves. God has seen him through all this craziness and turmoil and Jacob's response is thanksgiving and worship. Jacob simply set out to find a wife from among his cousins and ended up going through a lot over the last 20 years. But through it all Jacob knew the God of his father and grandfather was there with him every step.

Despite whatever uber-messed up family Jacob had, he was a godly man. He had a heart that beat for his God. Joseph had to see that modeled as he grew up and this unwavering faith modeled before him must have left a lasting impact on Joseph to see him through the darkness ahead.

IS there somebody that has wronged you that you need to go to this week to begin the healing? Don't let Satan get a foothold and drag you down by letting resentment and hurt to fester in your heart. Deal with it swiftly and pray fervently before you meet and God will bring healing.

34 Revenge

This chapter is one of the most messed up stories in scripture! There are several, but his is defiantly in the top 10. Genesis chapter 34 is the story of Dinah getting raped and then her brothers getting vengeance on the guy and his whole town for messing with their sister. Simeon was angry and he wanted revenge so they tricked the whole town of men to be circumcised. Verse 25 is one of the biggest understatements "they took their swords and entered to town without opposition." Then Simeon and Levi attacking a town full of freshly circumcised men killing them all! That is messed up! Brilliant, but messed up. This is just a glimpse of the depths of these brothers wickedness and their propensity toward violence, which will cost them their inheritance later. (Gen 49:5)

So what do you find most disturbing about this story? The Rape, the deceit or the savage revenge? What does this passage teach us? How about your desire for revenge, how does it affect you and your faith?

Three Funerals & A Birth

I love this call from Jacob to his household to purify themselves. To throw away any false gods that may have inadvertently or deliberately crept into their lives living in Paddan-Aram. Then they buried them under a tree. I wonder if anyone has ever tried to find the old tree in Shechem and used a metal detector like that old guy at the beach to find these old idols. (P.S. If I just inspired you to do that and you find something . . . I want my cut!)

After a long journey, they arrive and I love Jacob's priorities when he gets there. 1st thing Jacob does is build an altar to worship God. God gives Jacob a new start here at Bethel and turns the old deceiver Jacob into Israel. Not only that, God reveals a new name/character trait about himself to his beloved Israel El-Shaddai, which means God Almighty.

This is a transitional chapter from the long journey home, the death of the nurse, Jacob's beloved bride Rachel and his Father Isaac all die. And yet Jacob now transitioned to Israel knew ahead of all this unwanted change, that El Shaddai, God Almighty was in charge and was with him. This must have sustained him through his sorrows here.

Are there some "idols" (things getting in the way of worshiping God) in your life, you might need to throw out?

The Black sheep are blessed

Even though Esau and Ishmael were the "black sheep" of the family, God still kept his word to bless Ishmael's descendants. Here we see a glimpse of that through Basemath. What a great name for a band! Basemath. Well Basemath wasn't a band, but she was the daughter of Ishmael and had children through Esau. Basemath!

This chapter is the end of Esau and Jacobs story from here on we focus on Joseph. What have you learned about God through their story?

A coat, a dream, eBay and some hubba bubba

37

I dream a lot. I vividly remember my dreams and so does my daughter. Sometimes we share what we have dreamt with each other and most of the time our response is the same, "wow that one was really **crazy.**" She has yet to come and tell me that her sister and our dogs and mother will one day bow before her, which I'm thankful for, but it probably wouldn't go over too well in our house and we all like each other and get along.

So when 17 year old Joe, whose brothers "couldn't say a kind word to him," (verse 4) hear his dream, let's just say they didn't take it very well. These guys were already the product of the baby arms race and sibling rivalry isn't even close to the atmosphere in that family. To make things worse, Joe was daddy's favorite, which only amplified the hatred his brothers felt for him.

Shechem! Sounds like a made up Christian cuss word when you stumped your big toe on the lamp stand in the middle of the night. And as far as we've seen, this town is a bit of a nasty place. It's where Dinah was raped, and all the guys were tricked into circumcision, which is just not right, and then killed. It's where Jacob buries all the family idols by a tree and it's where Joseph's ½ brothers were supposed to be tending the flock.

Joseph's sweet coat was an eye soar for his jealous brothers and the site of Joseph in the distance stirred them to plot his death. But thanks to Joe's oldest ½ brother Reuben, they just threw him in a well and left him for dead. However, Judah was a screwed businessman and decided to sell their brother on eBay to some Hubba Bubba salesmen. (v25) Brilliant! And honestly how many of you wouldn't have wanted to trade your annoying brother or sister for a year's supply of

65

bubalicious gum! Grape, tootie fruity, cotton candy the flavors were too enticing! Who could say no to such a tempting trade!!

As we are introduced to Joe here in ch37 things go from everyday normal life for a teenager to his brothers beating him up and selling him into slavery quickly. Joseph's life was instantly turned upside down. That's just life. The really hard stuff in life comes on us quickly and unexpectedly like a sucker punch. And we look around, dazed and confused trying to make sense of it all. And there are really only 2 responses when life sucker punches you. 1. God what is your problem?! Why did you sucker punch me like this?! I thought you loved me?? Why would you allow this to happen to me?

And some take it a step further and lash out at God with "I hate you! You ruined my life!" And that's an honest first response to a tragedy in life. Cancer, the death of a close friend, divorce, the loss of your job, house, or spouse. Those are the kinds of deep hurts that can't be brushed over with a Hallmark card.

Our 2nd option is "God what are you doing?? Why did you allow this to happen? I don't know what you're doing but I have no choice but to trust you. I need you God. You gotta help me get through this. I really just want you to make it all go away, I don't want to learn anything else right now, and I'm hurting too badly. But you are my Rock and my refuge and I have nowhere else to turn but to you. Please God don't leave me. I need you!"

And it's from that place of desperation that I'm sure Joseph was feeling here at the end of 17 that leads us to the secret caverns of deep intimacy with God that we could never find on our own. You can't read a book about it or go to a seminar. The only secret path to that place of intimacy is through the tough road of suffering that leads us to the cross. I wish there was another way, a shortcut or something, but there isn't. I wish I could tell you, I got all that stuff I just said from some great guru book on pain and suffering etc, but that was all from my heart and the deep valleys God has walked me through in my life. Those were the questions I was asking and wrestling with and I'm pretty sure if you are in the middle of some tough stuff, you are probably asking the same questions.

Our hope, our only hope to make it through the tough stuff of life is to run to the Father. Crying, snot nosed, broken, grabbing him tightly, and knowing that He will never leave us or forsake us. He will never let go. He alone can sustain us and lift us up out of the pit, like Joseph. U2 does a great remix of David's song in Psalms 40 "I waited patiently for the Lord he inclined and heard my cry, he lift me up out of the pit, out of the miry clay. He set my feet upon the rock and made my footsteps firm, many will see, many will see and hear, and I will sing, sing a new song."

If you're like me, you probably would rather read about someone else going through tough stuff, like Joseph here, and "see what God has done and be encouraged." We would rather spectate when it comes to learning God's truths than go through anything uncomfortable. We want an easy button when it comes to learning, but that is not how God works and it's not how we learn best.

I've been through some tough stuff in my life and I would never want to do it again, the pain was too great. But I would **never** trade it for anything in the world. I would do it again the same way because of the intimacy it brought me with God. It doesn't go on forever, he will lift you up and steady your feet on the Rock and give you a new song to sing. I am living proof of that and so are the 1,000's of men and women in the Bible and the bazillions of people around the world throughout time.

What tough stuff are you facing right now that you need God's help? Take some time and just unload it all before the throne of God. He is faithful to carry you through whatever you are facing.

Warning! Do not read this chapter with small children! 38

(Ok, just a side note to begin here. God has a funny since of humor. Several times this year I've sat down with my 9th grade daughter at the breakfast table to read through Genesis. So I sit down today and open to Gen 38 and get ½ way through reading out loud and I slam on the brakes. "Uh, yeah I'm not reading the rest of this with you thing morning; let's skip over to 39." And the funny thing is about 5 months back we were doing the same thing reading through Genesis together and it was her day to read while I made breakfast and lunch and she was reading out loud and then slammed on the breaks. It seems inevitable that when I do that, some awkward passage about sex or Rachel with her "time of the month" would come up. I don't want to have that conversation at breakfast and those are "mom conversations." So we were both embarrassed and moved on to 39. (Call me a coward, I'm fine with that. God has a funny sense of humor!)

So Judah, the same guy who said "let's sell Joe," has a son with a Canaanite woman and I'm guessing he was sitting on the couch playing Xbox and his wife was trying to have a conversation with him about what to name the boy. His response was "Errr" and before he could complete his sentence "Errr, I don't know, whatever you want honey, let me finish this one game." She said, "Fine we'll name him Er." Yeah, I'm pretty sure that's how it happened.

Verse 7 is a bit shocking. It simply says Er was a wicked man so God decided to kill him. I'm not sure what he was into, his dad wasn't the nicest guy, mom was a Canaanite, and so it's not hard to imagine he was a bad man. But apparently, God dealt out his righteous judgment on Er & Onan for their wickedness.

Our God is a God of wrath and a God of love. We often don't like to talk about the wrath because we want the cuddly teddy bear God of love and puppies and rainbows. (Which were a sign of God's wrath sustained, but I digress) God is a just God. It is by his grace we all aren't in the same trouble Er was in. That doesn't make God mean, or weak, it makes him righteous. He shows His grace by sparing those of us who have been living in wickedness and rebellion.

This chapter highlights our depravity. After reading it my first response is simply "eww." Everything that went on was messed up and the fall of man is on full display and God's holiness shines brighter when we see the depths of our depravity.

There is always the temptation to live like your neighbors instead of like the people of God. Look at your life. Are you any different from you "Canaanite neighbors" Where has the truths of God impacted your life so much that you are different from our ungodly nation we are faced with today? If you are struggling to come up with differences in music and movie choices etc that should begin to reveal something to you.

Desperate Housewife = Run Forest Run!

I have always loved the story of Joseph! It's not because of all the action and fighting and things getting blown up—which is the typical story we find today in our culture. But Joseph's life story is one of unwavering trust in God. We don't even have Joseph's memoirs or many words of praise or sorrow like David's life in Psalms. There is this steadfast faithfulness that resonates off the pages when you read his life story. Here in 39 we catch up with Joseph as he is being sold by the bubble gum gang and an unknowing Egyptian officer buys him to wash his camels and mow the yard.

Potiphar had no idea of God's big picture plan to save the Israelites from famine by his simple purchase of a slave. Joseph had no idea his brothers beating him up and selling him into slavery would be used by God to redeem God's chosen people.

Joseph learned an awesome lesson in verse 2 and it is repeated throughout this chapter and his life. "The Lord was with Joseph." Does that help you to know that God was with/present/involved in his life? It does for me. When I look at the craziness of life and the hard times and the fun times to know God is tangibly present in my life floods my heart with peace.

And now for the desperate housewife. Maybe I like Joseph's story because I relate to verse 6 so much "Handsome, well built man." Yeah, I'm pretty sure that describes me. (And every other guy reading this in our own minds :) But the lesson of fortitude on Joseph's part is epic. "How could I sleep with you? It would be a sin against God." Joseph doesn't even care about Potiphar catching them, his Integrity runs deeper. I love verse 10 "he kept out of her way as much as possible." And when she finally got her filthy paws on him, he bolted!

Girls please FFWD to chapter 40; I need to talk to the guys for a second.

Guys how are you doing in this area of sexual temptation? Most of us are not daily tempted to sleep with another man's wife by her constant pleading with you. But some of you are flirting with a girl at work or school or online and your mind begins to plot and scheme about how you can be alone with her. Or most likely you're checking the latest news or sports on the web and you get enticed by a seductive image. She is calling your name, "_____ click on me," "Sleep with me," like Potiphar's wife calling.

What is your response here? Do you click on the image or do you respond like Joseph avoiding contact with websites or people for that matter that will tempt you. When that enticing image comes up, do you run like Joseph, close the computer, run the other direction from that woman who is tempting you or do you give in?

Job is an unlikely source for sexual purity, but I use a great line Job said to encourage my guy friends in this area of purity. Job 31:1 "I made a covenant with my eyes not to look with lust at a young woman." I'm sure Joseph had done that same thing and it's the only way you're going to make it through this life with integrity. You have to make a covenant in advance, stick to your covenant with the fortitude of Joseph and when temptation comes . . . Run Forest Run!

One Last teachable nugget from 39:20 Joseph is thrown in Jail for doing the right thing! Your pursuit of holiness will not always get you favor among men. But verse 21 The Lord was with Joseph and I'm pretty sure that is how you want your story to be written. Take just a minute to confess you sin/lust and make a covenant between you, your eyes and God. Memorize Job 31:1 and repeat it when temptation comes around, then RUN!

Pause for just a minute here and look at your life . . . are there things going on that maybe God is using to make a bigger impact than you know? Of course, like Joe, we don't see it until after key pieces of the Lego building are in place and we have a little bit of time in our rear view mirror. We need to get our minds thinking about the bigger picture plan that God may be wanting to use us for. Sometimes it helps to take our focus off the tiny pieces of life before us and ask God what is the big picture in all of this? What can I learn about God's character through all of this?

Twas the night before... 40

The prisoners were all snug in their beds while visions of sugarplums danced in their heads. Okay, so maybe there were no sugarplums, but there were grapes and the one dude had Twinkies on his head (verse 16).

RANDOM THOUGHT

You think your job stinks? The cupbearer's job was to serve drinks and not die. People were always trying to poison the king and this guy had to drink the wine first, and if he didn't die, then the king would drink. What a crappy job! It came with prestige etc, but who cares! You could get poisoned and die and that is no fun!

THGUOHT MODNAR

Despite having a stinky job, the cupbearer here with Joseph gets a good dream interpretation from Joseph. Joseph pleads with him to remember him when he gets out in 3 days, but he forgets Joseph.

The baker's dream of Twinkies stacked on his head however is not so good. I wish I could have seen the bakers face. I know it's a little twisted, but verse 16 says the baker heard the cupbearer's dream and was feeling pretty optimistic. 3 days and you will be "lifted up" and restored. So Joe is telling the baker the same deal, the baker is nodding along, excited "3 days, yeah! I'm going to be lifted up," sweet, just like the cupbearer and then insert the sound of tires screeching.

"Wait, what?! I'm going to be lifted up and impaled on a pole!!" Not only is this bad news, this dude has 3 days of no sleep and freaking out to do while he waits to be killed! Poor dude, he should have made little Debbie zebra cakes. Mmmmm Zebra Cakes.

Through it all, Joseph is forgotten by fickle men and left in prison, but not forgotten by God.

Have you ever felt like God forgot about you like we see Joseph forgotten for 2 years? What lesson do you think God might have been teaching Joseph?

Get out of Jail free

Two years is a long time to sit in prison for a crime you didn't commit! There's no need to fear, Super Cows are here! They parachute in and in verse 2; they walk up out of the river to save the day. Verse 14 is a reminder that this was no summer camp for Joseph. He was scruffy, stinky prisoner looking like Chewbacca after 2 years in prison so he gets a shave and a hair cut before meeting the king.

Despite being wrongfully imprisoned, Joseph has maintained his integrity. He could have gone to meet Pharaoh and told him **he** has the power to interpret dreams as a guaranteed way to get a get out of jail free card. But Joseph's reply to Pharaoh is "I can't help you, but God can." Isn't that our responsibility as Christians? When we are talking with friends or someone we've just met our conversations should turn toward God as the source of relief for whatever is concerning them.

Wow, what a crazy day for Joseph. He began his day like any other looking like a scruffy nurf herder and ending it dressed in royal clothes **and** got a wife! He is now 2nd in command with lots of bling and a sweet new chariot with 38" wheels! Verse 46 tells us that Joseph left Pharaoh's presence after being in Jail for many years and he went cruising in his new ride to "inspect the entire land of Egypt." Fresh out of Jail with his new lady friend he is in his chariot with his arm around her and they went cruising down the fast food strip. With a little further study, I was curious who Joseph's new wife was.

What kind of priest was her father? It says he was the priest of On. This wasn't referring to a light switch

RANDOM THOUGHT

Remember they had no electricity and no "on" light switches. Because if they did, I bet Jacob would have turned on the lights on his honey moon and seen Princess Leah and not Rachel and demanded a refund from the father in law. And I bet if they had light switches, Judah would have recognized Tamar and not slept with her! 2 things these guys need were lights and a good baby name book, because they make a mess of things so far without them!

So On ironically is not a reference to a light switch, but an ancient city in Egypt and the priest would have been worshiping the sun god Re. This city On, where Joseph's father in law was a priest; they had these big statues call obelisk in the city. And the crazy part as I was studying I found out that we have one of these actual statues right here in America! It's in central Park in NY! They have one there, I don't know why, but it's there.

See how fun studying God's word can be. I was just curious what kind of religious stuff the father-in-law might be teaching his PK daughter Asenath and the grandkids. And by looking at a bible dictionary and a few simple web searches for On and Obelisk you can find out all kinds of cool stuff!

THGUOHT MODNAR

Despite being blessed by God, being lifted up out of Prison and now VP of Egypt, you can still feel the deep pain Joseph felt through everything he had been through. Look at verse 51-52 and the names he gives his sons. He is still wrestling with the hurt of the betrayal of his brothers. I'm sure there were many, many days he was in prison that he thought if it weren't for his brothers, he wouldn't be here in Egypt in Jail. I'm sure he also had days he thought of ways he would get his revenge if he ever saw them again. Manasseh—God has made me forget everyone in my father's family, and Ephraim "in the land of my grief."

Even though Joseph knew God was with him and blessing him, the pain of life was still there. Everything wasn't all roses and tickle fights now that he is out of jail. The betrayal of his family still cut him deep and as the famine spread and people from around the world began to come for help, I wonder if Joseph began thinking of his family crawling to him for help. Whatever Joseph thought, God's thoughts were still focused on redemption. Keeping his covenant, saving the lineage of Noah and Abraham by building the nation of Israel through Joseph's hardship . . . add a brick.

Is there someone in your family who has hurt you deeply that you haven't completely forgiven? Take a minute to pray for that person and ask God to heal your heart.

We see part of God's big picture plan for Joseph's life bloom here as God blesses him with prestige and honor and new riches. God has brought Joseph a long way from that well his brothers beat him up and threw him in. Does this short glimpse of blessing bring you hope in the midst of your tough situation? I hope that it does.

DBLOH 6 1/2

As God's plan of redemption for his people and specifically Jacob and his family begins to unfold, we see Joseph messing with his brothers. I'm not sure if he was a prankster or if this was out of partial revenge. I lean toward the latter due to the naming of his kids "God has made me forget everyone in my father's family" and Joseph's own thoughts of his dream being fulfilled (verse 9). So I bet it felt good to get a little payback on his brothers and he accuse them of working for MI6 aka 006,006.5,008,009.

I love verse 24! The brothers were freaking out and blaming each other for what they did to Joseph and as Joseph listened to them he broke down. The pain and bitterness that had been building up for decades crumbled when he was finally face to face with his family who had betrayed him. Maybe up to this point Joseph was planning on killing his brothers and getting the revenge/justice for how they had wronged him. But before he could go any further, God broke his heart in verse 24

I'm not sure why Joseph chose Simeon. I looked and all I could find was he was 2nd born from Princess Leah. It was a nice touch tying him up in front of his brothers to put the fear into them and it obviously worked.

Verse 21 & 28 says something about the brother's theology. They were under the impression that God is a tricky vengeful god. They thought they were being punished for their betrayal of Joseph and then when they find the $ in the grain, they blame God! In all fairness to them, I guess that is a normal response. When things go awry in our lives, we are quick to point the finger at God. Sometimes there is sin in our lives that we deserve and need to be disciplined in order to repent. But often times, like the 9 band of brothers here, we get easily scared of our circumstances and focus so intently on the one puzzle piece of life before us, we can't see the big picture. These brothers couldn't see God using Joseph to bless his brothers and father through all this. They only had the moment before them and the same is true for you and me.

I would love to have a book about my life and family that I could read and know how things are going to turn out. Will I struggle financially? Will my daughters marry Godly men? Will I lose my job, my hair, my wife and will I become a hobo on roller skates in Miami Beach? 'cause let's be honest if I'm going to be a hobo, I want to be one where it's warm and I can work on my tan.

We all have fears and anxiety in life because we don't know how our story will unfold. But as Christians, believers in the God of the galaxies, we have those fears sustained. Note that I didn't say all our fears go away and everything is perfect. There is no "health and wealth" prosperity message in the life of Joseph. If that is what you see, you are missing the point of God's bigger plan. Joseph suffered for decades and through it all, God was with Joseph and he knew that God was with him and it sustained his fears and pain. God held Joseph up through it all and the God of Joseph is the same God who will hold you up and carry you through the tough stuff of life.

Would you like to a have the book of your life so you could see what was next? When someone does you wrong, what is your natural response? Revenge or do you try to work it out?

He's in the Jailhouse Now 43

Verse 2 is one of those verses that is easy to skip right over. I don't know how long it takes to travel from Hebron (35:27) to Egypt by donkey, but apparently, they didn't turn right back around to get Simeon. They left him in the jailhouse and now that the food was running out, they decided to do something! So there had to be at least several months that Simeon sat in jail in Egypt. Verse 10 Judah says they could have gone and returned twice which is a pretty good indicator this was not a weekend in the county lock up.

I find it interesting that Jacob wouldn't take Reuben up on his offer to sacrifice his own sons to go and save Simeon, but Jacob listened to Judah. Reuben was going to save Joseph from the well (37:29) and it was Judah's idea to sell Joseph to the bubble gum salesmen. (37:26-27)

Jacob finally realizes there is no way out of this so he tries to make the best plans he can to secure the return of all his sons. So he prepares a bountiful bribe/gift. Verse12 is funny because it is the first time we see a government worker getting blamed for a clerical error.

This is a great story of reunion for Joseph and Benjamin. When Joseph first sees Ben he tries to compose himself and he blessed him (verse 29) and then Joseph loses it and has to run out of the room. You can feel the deep love for his brother Benjamin and when it was dinner time he gave him extra giant turkey leg and they ate, drank but none of them were Mary. Because they were all dudes, but they were merry.

I wonder if Simeon learned anything during his time in Jail like Joseph did. What about you? What have you learned about God in your suffering?

Have you ever done something bad and gotten away with it? The brothers here think they have gotten away with what they did to Joseph and all is good with the banquet, but the truth always comes out. Perhaps this passage is an chance to remind you it's time to fess up to whatever it was you got away with before it comes to light in a bad way.

44 Magic 8 Ball

Joseph is quite the prankster. He uses the same trick as before, but this time he took it up a notch by putting the silver cup in Ben's bag. Then he messes with them and says "Don't you know this is the cup I tell the future with!" You stole my magic 8 ball! I'm not sure how he can keep a straight face in all this, but he has Judah quaking in his sandals. (vs16)

Yet despite his fear of this Egyptian ruler, Joseph, Judah is like Colin Raye's country song "That's my story and I'm sticking to it." Judah says Joseph is dead (verse 20) and it must have been the #1 cause of deaths in the Middle East . . . Bear attacks! (Verse 27)

And he completes his sob story with, "you wouldn't want to kill an old white haired man now would you?"

Despite Judah's shortcomings, he steps up here and gives a courageous speech to the Egyptian leader (Joseph). What about you? Is God calling you, like Judah, to do something honorable or courageous?

Candid camera/ you've been Punked! 45

"Joseph could stand it no longer." The pranks and trickery are now over, and they are about to learn that they have all been "punked" The brothers response to Joseph's unveiling was classic "they were stunned and speechless." I'm not sure if Judah wet his tunic here realizing his lies about the bear attack were ridiculous and Joseph had the power to destroy him.

Joseph saw God's big picture plan and he has to tell his brother repeatedly to ease their fear and tension in the room. I'm sure they felt like they were about to get it from Joseph, but Joseph says "It was God who sent me here and not you!" The deep hurt and pain of family betrayal had washed away with their tears as they embraced one another. Joseph was able to forgive his brother because of the peace God gave Joseph. Joseph had many years of hardship, isolation from his family, slavery, imprisonment and then suddenly going from jail to VP of Egypt. And just as suddenly, Joseph's brother show up to get some tacos. It's neat to watch the life of Joseph unfold here with his brothers. There had to be this inner conflict for Joseph to say "I told you that you would bow before me, now clean my toe nails!" I'm sure there had to part of him that wanted revenge for all he had been through at the hands of his brothers and especially Judah.

But God wouldn't allow the bitterness to fester in Joseph's heart. You can see the hard process of forgiving someone who had wronged him only through the knowledge of the sovereignty of God.

I don't know if you have ever been betrayed by someone close to you, but it hurts. Deeply. This is not something you can simply "shake off" overnight. We are called to forgive those that have wronged us in light of the forgiveness we have received from Christ (Col 3:13) and most of us know that, but sometimes forgiveness is tough.

I have always tried to have a forgive-forget policy. Once I say "I forgive you," I will forever forget it and never bring it back up. I try to not bring up old hurts with my wife so we can heal and grow beyond our mistakes. It has been easier with her because of the mutual love we have for each other. But there have been people in my life who have sought to harm me and hurt me. They were close as a brother and then betrayed me. They sought their own gain with no thought of the pain it would bring me and my family. Much like Judah and his brothers did toward Joseph. Those are the deep wounds that are tough to mend. It takes longer to heal and sometimes the smallest thing can open the wound up again and the healing process has to start over.

I used to believe I was able to instantly forgive-forget any wrong and move on. I have found with the hard road of life, sometimes forgiveness is a cyclical process. By cyclical I mean you forgive someone for the pain they have caused you. You confess you sin to God and ask for healing and you receive peace from God. A real sense of healing and closure and restoration, and then something happens to remind you of the betrayal and you begin the process of forgiving again.

I'm not telling you this is how you ought to live your life; I'm just trying to be real with the process of healing that can sometimes take time. But like we see with Joseph, God is able to erode any grudge Joseph may have built up over the years. That is my prayer for me and for you. I can tell you I have truly forgiven the 1st person, who betrayed me, but the messed up part of life is then I met a different person who wounded me and the process began all over with them. Our lives can be full of hurtful people and we can become jaded grumpy old men, or we can ask God to teach us, heal us, and help us to forgive and truly love those that wound us.

In light of Colossians 3:13 (NLT)

Make allowance for each other's faults, and forgive anyone who offends you. Remember, the Lord forgave you, so you must forgive others.

Who do you need to forgive today?

Are we there yet?? 46

We are fascinated today with people who have more than 2.5 children. John & Kate +8, The Dugger's with their 20+ kids (Probably 30 by the time you read this!) But if there was a reality TV show around when Jacob was leaving Beersheba to Egypt they would have been fixed on Jacob and his **70** kids and grandkids!

I have a tough time traveling to Disney with my wife and two daughters making it 4 exits down the interstate before somebody has to stop for a potty break! I can't imagine trying to move 70 kids and grandkids by donkey more than 400 miles!

הגענו כבר?

That is Hebrew for "Are we there yet?" Which I'm sure Jacob heard a bazillion times on this long journey with that many kids. I'm not great with math so someone figure this out for me and I'll buy you a taco and put it in the 10-year anniversary hardback edition of this book. There is an algebra problem hiding here see if you can figure it out. Verse27 says Jacob had 70 descendants and by the time, the Israelites leave Egypt 400 years later they had 2.5 million people all from this one family of 70. So how many kids/ grandkids did each son of Jacob have?

Anywho, that was a big family for Jacob to move to Egypt! As they approached Goshen Jacob asked Judah to do something so vial as a man I can barely bring my fingers to type to recount the horrifying and disturbing details. Verse 28 **He stopped to ask for directions**! Dunt dunt duuuh! Ha ha, you thought it was going to be something really bad didn't you. Moses never stopped to ask for directions and that's why they wandered in the desert for 40 years. Bud dump bump ching! Ok, I'm sorry; I told you I hang around middle and high school guys way too much!

Finally, after a long journey and many years apart Joseph and Jacob are reunited with lots of tears and hugging. What a great story of a son thought dead and now reunited with his father and family. How has Lifetime or Hallmark not made a cheesy afterschool special with this plot yet?

Before we leave this chapter, this last verse confused me at first. Joseph tells his family to tell Pharaoh they are shepherds. Which is fine and good until he says "the Egyptians hate shepherds." So why would you tell Pharaoh your family is a bunch of shepherds?? Won't he say "Eww shepherds are gross" and turn them away? No, it wasn't that bad of a profession, some people say Joseph did this so they would have a bit of privacy and not be bothered to intermarry etc which makes more sense. I also find it Ironic that God chose to reveal Jesus the savior of humanity to who?? Yep, shepherds. (But that's another story for Volume 34 of this book series due out Christmas 2044, so look for it on your Cranium download.)

We see God calling Jacob to go to down to Egypt and Jacob replies "Here I am" Just like Abraham.

What is God calling you to and is your response the same as Jacobs? Maybe you never thought to commit your future to God's steady hands. Take a minute to give your future plans to God and ask Him to give you a malleable heart like Jacob so that you can say "Here I am."

I said a Pharaoh Pharoah

Jacob goes with Joseph to meet Pharaoh and verse 7 is funny to me. Imagine you get to go meet the President or Supreme Chancellor of your day. It's an honor, a big deal, they probably had to go through a lot of security, like Pharaoh's guards, an invasive pat down, metal detector, Cat scan . . . get it, Cat scan 'cause the Egyptian liked cats so much. I'm sorry about that one, it was extra corny. I promise it won't happen again!

So they go in to meet this all-powerful important man and it doesn't go like I would expect. You might expect the King to look down to the lowly Hebrew and say some kind words or something, but nope. As soon as Jacob meets Pharaoh, Jacob blessed Pharaoh! How awesome is that! You might expect it to go the other way around, but honestly what could Pharaoh have blessed Jacob with? Pharaoh was most likely a worshiper of the sun god Re, so the only blessing he could have offered may have been "May my god Re give you a deep dark tropical tan." While Jacob's God was the God of the universe who had mucho power over all of creation including the sun and the stars. So it isn't that odd after you think about if for the blessing to flow from Jacob to Pharaoh because that is the only direction it could go. So Jacob blessed Pharaoh, **twice.**

Joseph was a master economist and Chairman of the Egyptian Federal Reserve. Literally because he was responsible for all the food saved up in the **reserve** and now he was passing it out. The Egyptians eventually ran out of horses and $$ and land to offer Pharaoh for food until they had given it all and Pharaoh now owned everything. He had all the $, livestock, land and all the people and you thought your taxes were bad! This was the greatest land acquisition before the Louisiana Purchase! But there was an exception to all of this. Who still had all their livestock, land and freedom? The Israelites and the Priest of Re.

As chapter 47 closes, we see that awkward handshake again "put your hand under my thigh and swear." Can you see bankers and businessmen doing that today? Ha!

Joseph was a hard worker and God blessed him and the entire nation of Egypt through Joseph. Are you a hard worker? Do your parents, teachers, or boss notice you work hard all for the glory of God?

criss cross 48

It is fun to see Jacob here at the end of his life with much joy being able to bless his son Joseph and his grandsons. I also think even at the age of 147 he was still sharp. When it came time to give out the blessing, he waited for Joseph to get the boys all situated how Joseph wanted to receive the blessing. The oldest boy was on the right hand of Jacob and the younger boy on the left. But I don't think Jacob was too old to remember the trick he played on his dad Isaac, so right before blessing them he crossed his arms! Ha, Joseph was outwitted by a 147-year-old man.

What a great testimony of a Godly family in this blessing that Jacob gives. Can you feel the intimacy between God and this family? Jacob remembers the lessons about God and His faithfulness to his grandfather Abraham and his dad Isaac. And the loving care and protection God gave to Jacob as a shepherd lovingly cares and provides for his sheep.

Joseph tried to correct Jacob and switch hands but Jacob knew what he was doing. The promises of God fulfilled through Jacob and Joseph are wonderful. Manasseh will become a great people and Ephraim's descendants will become many great nations. And through it all "God will be with you." A lesson no one needed to tell Joseph about as he knew it firsthand. God was with him through his life and he could be assured of God's continual presence among his descendants.

What is your favorite memory of your grandparents? Check out Hebrews 11:21 to see what it says about Jacob as a man of faith. Why do you think out of his life of 147 years this one event stands out?

Blessings & Honor 49

Jacob, AKA Israel, calls the whole family together to dispense his final blessing and it doesn't go as you might think. Reuben was to receive the privilege of the 1st born son, but he had sex with his step mom. Simeon and Levi were rambunctious and played too many violent video games and they disqualified themselves with the slaughter of Shechem and the other men of the village. Judah is the one who gets the best blessing. Yeah the same Judah who said "let's sell little Joey." Maybe Joseph never ratted his brother out to their dad when they were reunited in Egypt, I don't know. Whatever the case, God chose to carry His promise through the line of Judah (verse 10) foretelling of Christ's eternal reign.

Then there was Zebulun the sailor man toot toot, Issachar the sturdy Donkey, Vote for Governor Dan a politician you can trust. Half way through as Jacob is looking at his 12 boys he says in verse 18, "I trust in you for salvation O Lord!" I'm not sure if this was like saying "God these are a bunch of messed up jokers and I know you said you would make a great nation, but I don't know how you're gonna do it with this rag tag bunch, but . . . I trust in you for salvation O Lord!" That seems to fit nicely with the addition of the exclamation mark. I'm pretty sure that was how he was feeling. If it was a reminder for the boys to remember to trust in God's salvation, there would be no need for the passionate punctuation!

Gad, you're going to get mugged, Asher will become the next Top Chef, Naphtali was really, really ridiculously good looking and probably the first male model with looks like Blue steel, Ferrari or Le Tigre.

Joseph gets the birthright from Jacob (FFWD to 1 Chronicles 5:2) for all he has been through. We get new names for God here in verse 24 Mighty One, Shepherd, and The Rock of Israel. I don't think we spend enough time remembering the names God gives us in his Word that describes Him. Other smart people have gone through scripture and counted and they came up with 120 names, titles, descriptions and metaphors of God.

After pointing his boys toward God and blessing them, he "drew his feet into bed and joined his ancestors." What a great fulfilling life Jacob lived in life and Godly heritage he left in his death. The greatest hope we find here is not in the future of Jacob's sons, but the hope of life eternal as we pass from this life into eternity with our family that has gone on before us.

Read 49:10-12 again. Who is the descendant of Judah? Hebrews 7:14-17 gives it away.

Battle of the Bones

What a great testament to the life of integrity Joseph led by Pharaoh letting him return to Canaan. Not only return, but it was attended by all the Egyptian dignitaries. They didn't know Jacob, but they respected Joseph and owed him and his God their very lives. The funeral procession had to be in the hundreds as they returned Jacob's body to be with his Father and Grandfather and the rest of his family.

You may be wondering, like I was, if they ever found that cave with all the fathers of our faith. And the answer is yes. Herod the Great built some walls around it to protect it, but these patriarchs have defiantly not been able to R.I.P. (Even though they aren't there, it's just their bones) From Muslims to Crusaders and Jews there has been much bloodshed over this site of the cave for 1000's of year's right up to today!

After Jacob died, the 10 brothers feared Joseph's revenge would now fall on them and once again, Joseph became leaky. (Verse 17) And then the epic conclusion to this story comes with Joseph pointing to God's sovereignty in all of life. "You intended to harm me, but God intended it all for good." I hope that one short sentence brings you comfort as you struggle through some of the tough stuff of life. There will always be mean people who do bad things because we live in a fallen world. The dominoes of our depravity have been falling all throughout this book of Genesis from Eve to Adam to Cain on and on right up to the end of Genesis. (And right up to today too.) But if there is one thing that is woven through out Genesis as much as our depravity, it is the reassuring promise of God's intimate relentless pursuit of man.

Thanks for going with me on this journey through Genesis. Stay hungry for God's Word and keep your nose in it. Someone once said

"This book (the Bible) will keep you from sin or sin will keep you from this book."

Tune in next time, same Bat time, same Bat channel for EXODUS—movement of ya people.

Appendix

And now as Paul Harvey would say . . . The rest of the story.

Well we end our time together by coming full circle back to Genesis 1. We have seen how God reveals Himself to us through the beauty of his creation around us. God tells us He exists and tells us about Himself in His words to us the Bible. We've seen our response to God's gift of creation that He prepared for us by living in open rebellion and in sin. (Gen 3)

We have seen God's response by continuing to pursue us to guide us and build our faith. Like Abraham and that He is with us in our deep times of fear and pain like Joseph. John chapter 1:1-18 is a great chapter to bring things together. Jesus has revealed God to us. The final way we see God here is through the person of Jesus Christ. The incarnation, the visited planet of God coming to us in human flesh.

We began our journey together in Genesis looking at the question where was God before He made earth and the answer is the same, He is eternal, He always existed. John tells us here that the Word, which is Jesus, created everything. He spoke and by his Word, everything came into being except us. We were created by God, handmade in His image! And God breathed life into us.

John tells us before the beginning, Jesus existed and Jesus was with God and Jesus was God. Remember back in Gen 1:27 the "let us make man in our image" is a reference to the trinity. Verse 4 says the Word gave life to everything and everything was created through him. Then John shifts his analogy from the Word to the light. Remember out of a dark void came this light bursting on the scene in Genesis 1? And that's what we have with Jesus, a bright light bursting on to the scene. Some people think that God created us and then we sinned in Genesis 3 and God didn't plan for that so he had to make a backup plan and that was Jesus.

But the truth is, God's plan of redemption preceded our disobedience. It wasn't an afterthought. The divine trinity planned our redemption. In Genesis 3 right after our rejection of God, He provides clothes and a blood sacrifice that we see as a foreshadowing of Jesus' death and bloodshed to cleanse our sins.

Ephesians 1:4 God's people, you were chosen before all this was created! How awesome is that! Have you ever thought about that? You were chosen by God to be on His side before anything was created by his Grace alone. We see Jesus tells us about God's plan of redeeming us in his prayer right before he was crucified in John 17:1-7. "I have revealed you to the ones you gave me before the world even began" He ends the prayer in verse 25-26 then your love for me will be in them and I will be in them.

Acts 2:23, 24 Jesus' death was not an accident, the light could not be extinguished! God didn't create the world because he was bored or lonely. He created everything so that He could share his love with creatures who were made in the image of God and can respond willingly to his love.

Paul does an amazing job in Ephesians of telling the whole story of God's pursuit of us and God's plan of bringing you and me back into intimate fellowship with him before the fall, before we ran from God. Let's read Ephesians 1:2-14 now. As you read, look for the Trinity in this passage. We were chosen by God the father verse 3-6, purchased by the son verse 7-12 and sealed by the spirit verse 13-14. All of this is to praise and glorify God and the result is you and I get adopted by God and we have the gift of living in eternity with God and all this wasn't a big mistake, it was God's plan before there was ever a world!

Works Cited

Warren W. Wiersbe, *The Bible Exposition Commentary—Pentateuch*, (Colorado Springs, CO: Victor, 2001), WORD*search* CROSS e-book, 10.